THE GREATEST
MANIFESTATION
BOOK

THE RISING CIRCLE

We are an empowering wellness community dedicated to uplifting your vibration and supporting your inward journey. Our wide range of tools, resources and transformative products are thoughtfully curated to enhance your overall well-being.

Like an infinite circle, our spiritual journey has no beginning or end. We continue to expand and evolve, embracing the ever-unfolding possibilities. And just as the sun faithfully rises each day, the radiant light within us also awakens to illuminate our world.

As a compassionate community, we wholeheartedly believe in our collective capacity to rise and shine, co-creating a world brimming with love, understanding, and positive transformation.

Follow us on Instagram and TikTok @TheRisingCircle

Sign up to our weekly newsletter on www.therisingcircle.com

Get in touch via hello@therisingcircle.com

THE GREATEST MANIFESTATION BOOK

IS THE ONE WRITTEN BY YOU

The Rising Circle
Vex King and Kaushal

bluebird
books for life

First published 2023 by Bluebird
an imprint of Pan Macmillan
The Smithson, 6 Briset Street, London EC1M 5NR
EU representative: Macmillan Publishers Ireland Ltd, 1st Floor,
The Liffey Trust Centre, 117–126 Sheriff Street Upper,
Dublin 1, D01 YC43
Associated companies throughout the world
www.panmacmillan.com

ISBN 9781035030781

1 3 5 7 9 8 6 4 2

A CIP catalogue record for this book is available from the British Library.
Design and typesetting by Heather Bowen
Illustrations pp 49, 86, 89, 125, 133, 149, 185, 229 and 269 © Atomic Squib.
All other illustrations by Heather Bowen or Shutterstock.
Printed and bound in China

Visit www.panmacmillan.com/bluebird to read more about all our books
and to buy them. You will also find features, author interviews and
news of any author events, and you can sign up for e-newsletters
so that you're always first to hear about our new releases.

A MESSAGE JUST FOR YOU

We are proud of you for beginning this manifesting journey. Sometimes, manifesting can seem hard to get your head around, so we created *The Greatest Manifestation Book*, a daily journal to help you manifest your ideal life by working alongside your dreams, wishes and goals for the next six months.

This journal offers a simple yet exciting approach to manifestation. Each day you will have an opportunity to say a powerful affirmation, dig deep with a gratitude prompt, rewrite your manifesto, work on your limiting beliefs, raise your vibration, and engage with some great activities that will help you on your journey.

It brings us so much happiness to share this creation with all of you. We hope it sparks as much joy for you as it has for us.

With love,
Vex and Kaushal

This manifestation journal is dedicated to you.

Embark on this journey of raising your vibrations and getting closer to your dreams.

Now is the time to let go of limiting beliefs, fill your heart with gratitude, and manifest the life you deserve.

You've got this.

My name is

. . . and my manifestations are on the way.

CONTENTS

MANIFESTING 101

Everything you need to know about manifesting

WHAT IS MANIFESTING?

Manifesting is our ability to shape our experiential reality. Encouraging a positive attitude can attract more positivity into our lives. Often labelled the Law of Attraction (or Law of Vibration), this concept has recently gained more popularity as it offers a practical framework to channel your energy. At its core, the law suggests that you can achieve your biggest goals by consistently holding uplifting thoughts, speaking empowering words, boosting your mood, and taking action with intention.

Esther and Jerry Hicks are well-known authors and speakers on the Law of Attraction, from the teachings of the non-physical intelligence they define as 'Abraham'. Abraham tells us we can create our reality through our thoughts and beliefs and emphasizes the importance of aligning our thoughts and emotions with what we wish to experience. By focusing on positive feelings such as happiness and gratitude, we can attract more circumstances and events that return those feelings to us.

All emotions or feelings vibrate at a certain energy level (known as frequency) and can be ranked on a frequency scale. The highest and most powerful emotions are at the top: love, joy and peace. In contrast, the lowest frequency states are at the bottom, and they include insecurity, guilt and fear. To manifest what we desire, we need to vibe as high as possible by climbing up the frequency ladder.

According to the teaching of Abraham, our feelings serve as a guidance system that can help us understand whether we are in or out of alignment with our desires. So, it is important to pay attention to our emotions (use the highest/lowest vibe diagram opposite as a guide).

This journal will show you how to process and let go of limiting beliefs and negative thought patterns that hold you back from achieving your wishes, and will help you create a more fulfilling and wholesome life.

HIGHEST VIBE

LOVE
JOY
PEACE
GRATITUDE
EMPOWERMENT
HAPPINESS
ENTHUSIASM
OPTIMISM
HOPEFULNESS
CONTENTMENT

NEUTRAL

BOREDOM
FRUSTRATION
OVERWHELM
SADNESS
WORRY
ANGER
HATE
JEALOUSY
INSECURITY
GUILT
FEAR

LOWEST VIBE

WHO IS MANIFESTING FOR?

Manifesting is for anyone who wants to create positive changes in their life, and there are no limitations to this! Cultivating a manifesting mindset will go a long way, and we will teach you some game-changing techniques to encourage this way of thinking as you work your way through this journal.

HOW TO MANIFEST

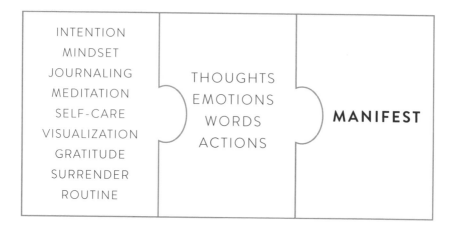

INTENTION
MINDSET
JOURNALING
MEDITATION
SELF-CARE
VISUALIZATION
GRATITUDE
SURRENDER
ROUTINE

THOUGHTS
EMOTIONS
WORDS
ACTIONS

MANIFEST

To manifest successfully, it is crucial to establish a solid foundation that aligns your vibrations with your wishes, dreams and desires. These include:

INTENTION	MEDITATION	GRATITUDE
MINDSET	SELF-CARE	SURRENDER
JOURNALING	VISUALIZATION	ROUTINE

By consistently working on these building blocks, you will pave the way towards your ideal life and maintain high vibrational levels. As a result, you will start noticing subtle changes in your thoughts, emotions, words and actions, which will gradually become ingrained in who you are.

Once you have these first two puzzle pieces in place, you will be well on your way to becoming closer to whatever you wish to manifest.

INTENTION
Set a clear intention for what you want to manifest. Your intentions should be positive, specific and aligned with your values.

MINDSET
Embrace a positive mindset to raise your vibrational energy and attract more favourable circumstances into your life.

JOURNALING
Use this journal to help you focus on the things you are grateful for in all areas of your life. Use the manifesting activities to support your journey. Doing so will cultivate a gratitude mindset and uplift your mood, creating a happier version of yourself.

MEDITATION
Regular meditation helps focus and align thoughts and emotions towards desired outcomes. It also enables you to raise your emotional state by letting go of that which does not serve you.

SELF-CARE
Practise self-care and prioritize your well-being. Taking care of your mind, body and spirit will help you protect your mental health and boost positive emotions.

VISUALIZATION
Visualize your desires as if they have already come true. Use your senses to create a clear and precise mental picture of what you want. You can use a vision board to help you or simply focus on your outcome using your imagination regularly.

GRATITUDE
Practise gratitude and take a moment to appreciate what you already have. When you count your blessings, you attract more.

SURRENDER
Trust in the Universe to provide for you. Let go of the need to control every aspect of the manifestation process. Seeking control can create limitations or breed doubt and fear, both of which create resistance to your goals.

ROUTINE
Establish a routine and try to make it a consistent habit of focusing on your desires and taking action towards them. It can also help you to manage your time more effectively and prioritize activities that align with your goals.

HIGH VIBE HACKS

Hacks to help keep you on track

MY HIGH VIBE HACKS KIT

This is the perfect page to turn to whenever you need a 'pick-me-up'. These will become your go-tos, to give your vibrations a much-needed boost!

Simply pick from the options below or write things that personally help you feel better in the boxes on the opposite page. The next time you are going through a bad patch or feeling sad, all you have to do is come back to this page and pick an activity to help you elevate your mood and feel aligned with your desires.

MEDITATE

Take this time to do a manifesting meditation to raise your vibrations.

SAY THANKS

Do not forget to have gratitude in your heart. Think of three things that you are grateful for right now.

REFRESH YOUR VISION

Look at your vision board and imagine a positive scenario using all five of your senses.

CLEAN THE AIR

Use your favourite crystal, sacred smoke or a singing bowl to enhance your space and energy.

MIRROR IT

Say your manifesto out loud to yourself in front of a mirror to feel the full effect of the words.

MANIFESTO MEMO

Listen back to your manifestation memo on your phone to help you stay focused on the bigger picture and raise those vibes (page 53).

SWAP IT

The words we speak hold vibrations, so consider using these swaps the next time you need some help.

I can't = I CAN

I think = I AM

I'm not good at this = I ALWAYS DO MY BEST

Why is this happening to me? = THIS WILL HELP ME GROW

MY PERSONAL HACKS

Use the boxes below to write down your own unique high vibe hacks to help you raise your energy!

HOW DO I USE THIS JOURNAL?

A simple step-by-step guide on how to use this journal

TODAY IS

Start each entry by writing down the date. By doing this you can go back to see how you were feeling on that specific day. Looking back on your entries is a great way to see how far you have progressed!

TODAY IS *Thursday 25th January 2024*

I AM CONFIDENT

AFFIRMATION

The words we say hold so much power over how we feel and are a crucial part of keeping your vibrations high. After the date, read the daily affirmation out loud five times for maximum effect!

WHAT IS MY VIBE LIKE TODAY?

As mentioned earlier, your vibration is key when it comes to manifesting. Here we have a barometer for you to fill in. Think of this as a visual representation of how you are feeling on that particular day. This is a helpful way to express your vibrations without using any words. It is also a useful tool for self-reflection and tracking your progress.

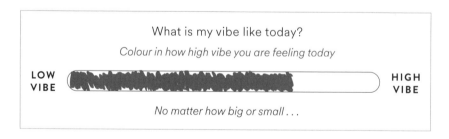

What is my vibe like today?

Colour in how high vibe you are feeling today

LOW VIBE — HIGH VIBE

No matter how big or small . . .

NO MATTER HOW BIG OR SMALL

It is important to point out that everything you write in your manifesting journal is valid. Accessing thoughts and emotions through the form of journaling helps you to let go of energies that no longer serve you, ultimately helping you in your manifestations.

GRATITUDE IS THE ATTITUDE

On every entry page, you will be asked one gratitude-led question which is an important pillar in your manifestation journey. These prompts will allow you to show appreciation of all the good in your life. The more gratitude we show, the more we receive to be grateful about. Writing down your blessings in life is a beautiful way to raise your vibe and lift your mood.

MY MANIFESTO

Your manifesto is what you want to manifest in a few sentences. The next chapter will show you exactly how to create this. It is important to feel every word you write down, to ensure that your vibrations are matching your words and so the Universe can get to work.

MY MANIFESTO

I am grateful for my health. I love my job and am so lucky and honoured that I get to do what I love and get paid for it. My friendships are flourishing and I am so happy! I am unstoppable!

VISUALIZE, SELF-CARE, POSITIVE TALK

Are you doing the groundwork every day to help you stay on track with your manifesting journey? These simple tick boxes serve as a reminder to visualize, carry out an act of self-care, and speak to yourself with positivity and kindness daily.

> Today I have done the below to support my journey . . .
>
> VISUALIZE   SELF-CARE   POSITIVE TALK

Here are some examples to get you going:

VISUALIZE	SELF-CARE	POSITIVE TALK
Meditate on your goal, look at your vision board, refresh your vision board.	Do something that brings you joy or calm like reading your favourite book.	Repeat positive affirmations that encourage you to speak to yourself with kindness, or try mirror work.

LET IT GO

Last but not least, it is time to let go and release anything that has been on your mind. This could be something that has happened that day, a limiting belief that is hindering you, or simply something you want to get off your chest. This is a powerful method for releasing anything that does not serve you. This is your safe space to let it all out to help you stay on track!

> Today I need to let go of . . .
>
> *feeling the need to make everyone happy. I need to make sure I put my happiness in the driving seat as this will help me in the long run* . . . to help me manifest.

HIGH VIBE ACTIVITIES

There will be different types of manifesting activities for you to do every three days to help you stay aligned on your journey.

MY FUTURE SELF

It is time to meet your future self! In each box, describe what your future self has achieved. Believe in everything you write down and visualize it already happening. Let's go!

LIFE	CAREER

LOVE	FINANCE

30-DAY MANIFEST CHECK-IN

Self-reflection is important, as this will show any areas where you are doing well and any aspects that may need improvement. You will be asked specific questions every thirty days to help you stay on track with your manifestations.

MY MANIFESTO

How to create your written vision to help you stay focused

MANIFEST YOUR INTENTIONS

In order to manifest intentionally, you must be specific about what you want. Similar to finding a specific location, knowing the precise zip code or coordinates is crucial to reaching your destination. Now is the time to get serious and drill into your desires.

OVERCOME LIMITING BELIEFS

Let's start by addressing limiting beliefs, as they play a crucial role in shaping our reality. Negative thoughts can act as obstacles that prevent us from achieving our goals and dreams, and they may also lower our vibration, making it difficult to experience the desired emotions associated with our desires. Therefore, it is important to make some adjustments by swapping out those limiting beliefs for more empowering ones.

BELIEF #1	SWAP

BELIEF #2	SWAP

BELIEF #3	SWAP

WHAT DO YOU WANT TO MANIFEST?

HOW DO YOU WANT TO FEEL?

WHAT IS YOUR WHY?

HOW TO WRITE YOUR MANIFESTO

Use the answers to the questions above to write your own unique manifesto. Include at least three things you would like to manifest and how you would feel by having those three things in your life – and make sure you write it in the present tense.

MY MANIFESTO

Use the box below to write your manifesto. You can always change and adapt along the way. Use the notes section at the back of the journal to do this.

MY MANIFESTO

MY ROUTINE AND NON-NEGOTIABLES

How to get your time to work for you and your manifestations

Having a routine adds structure to your day, which helps you to be more productive and focused on your manifesting journey. You do not need to overthink or complicate your routine – in fact, simplicity is key. If you wish, you can slowly add to it over time, working with what benefits you most.

MY MORNING ROUTINE

What you do in the morning can help set the tone for the rest of your day. Making your bed every morning, meditating or journaling are just some of the healthy habits that will start your day on a positive note and cultivate a more productive attitude that aligns with your goals and aspirations.

MY EVENING ROUTINE

Your evening routine is just as important as your morning one, as it allows your mind and body to slow down before sleeping. Doing something as simple as reading a book for twenty minutes every evening, staying away from screens, or doing evening stretches will help you switch off for the day.

Use the boxes below to create your routines:

MY MORNING ROUTINE

MY EVENING ROUTINE

NON-NEGOTIABLES

Your non-negotiables are the tasks and activities that are important to you. These are the things you will not compromise on and will ensure you make time for. By making these regular habits, no matter your personal or surrounding circumstances, you will find it easier to set boundaries and intentions, and get closer to manifesting your dreams, goals and wishes.

THE 1-1-1 METHOD

At The Rising Circle, we all live by The 1-1-1 Method, in which you create three non-negotiables that you must do for yourself and your well-being – one every day, one every week, and one every month. For example:

1 DAILY NON-NEGOTIABLE

Eat your breakfast without using your phone
Spend a couple of mindful minutes doing your skincare routine

1 WEEKLY NON-NEGOTIABLE

Cook your favourite meal
Have a self-care hour

1 MONTHLY NON-NEGOTIABLE

Have a catch-up call with your best friend
Treat yourself to a solo date

Write your non-negotiables below:

---

1 THING I WILL DO EVERY DAY FOR MYSELF

1 THING I WILL DO EVERY WEEK FOR MYSELF

1 THING I WILL DO EVERY MONTH FOR MYSELF

VISION BOARD 101

Everything you need to know about creating a vision board

WHAT IS A VISION BOARD?

A vision board is a creative tool that curates your deepest desires and aspirations through pictures, words and symbols.

Not only does the human brain process visual information faster than any other type of information, but consistently embedding inspiring images into your subconscious will open your conscious awareness to opportunities that attract the manifestations.

If you were to have a picture of a dream travel destination that you wake up and look at every day, your mind will continuously search for confirmation that this holiday is happening. With this image nestled in the back of your mind, the front of your mind begins to form the perfect circumstances to align you with the chance to travel.

There is no wrong way to create a vision board. You may prefer a physical board with cut-out images or a digital version on Canva (an online graphic design tool).

HOW DO I MAKE A VISION BOARD?

We are going to share a simple four-step guide on the best way to create your vision board. We recommend taking a picture of it on your phone, too, so you always have it handy.

1. PREP AND SET

Prep your equipment. Do you need a printer? Magazines? Pens and pencils? Are you going to draw? Or design digitally? Make sure you have everything you need before you get started. Set the scene with candles or crystals to get you in the mood.

2. GET INTO THE ZONE

To bring your vibrations up, try doing a little meditation or breathwork before starting, or putting on your favourite playlist in the background and making yourself a nice warm drink.

3. PICK YOUR TIMELINE + CATEGORIES

It is important to pick categories and a timeline for your vision board. We recommend creating a vision board for the next six months and updating it as and when needed. If you are looking for inspiration on how to pick categories for your vision board, try these examples: goals, love, life, personal development, fitness, home, health, relationships, career, travel, spiritual and hobbies.

4. CURATE YOUR LIFE

Now is the time to physically create your vision board. The most important thing is to select words, images and symbols that evoke the strongest emotional response every time you focus on them. And remember: no dream is too big when it comes to this!

REMINDER TO MYSELF

What to remember when you feel stuck

We can be our own worst critics at the best of times. It is OK to miss a day, to not be in the mood or to take a break for a bit. Allow room for flexibility and practise self-compassion to protect your vibes.

Just remember that if you ever take a step back, you can still step forward again and resume your practice. This manifestation journal will always be here to help you in your journey.

To remind you of this, fill in and sign a little promise to yourself below.

A PROMISE TO MYSELF

I _____ hereby agree that I will not be hard on myself if I miss a day's entry and will try my best to pick up where I left off when I am ready. I also promise myself that . . .

IF I GET FRUSTRATED, I WILL

_____

IF THINGS DO NOT GO TO PLAN, I WILL

_____

IF I MISS A DAY OF JOURNALING, I WILL

_____

Signed _____

Date _____

MY
MANIFESTATION
JOURNAL

I AM CONFIDENT

What is my vibe like today?

Colour in how high vibe you are feeling today

LOW VIBE ⊂─────────────────────────────⊃ **HIGH VIBE**

No matter how big or small . . .

What is something I am thankful for in my life right now and why?

_____

_____

_____

MY MANIFESTO

_____

_____

_____

_____

Today I have done the below to support my journey . . .

VISUALIZE ●   SELF-CARE ●   POSITIVE TALK ●

Today I need to let go of . . .

_____

_____

. . . to help me manifest.

I AM RESILIENT

What is my vibe like today?

Colour in how high vibe you are feeling today

LOW VIBE ⟨_____⟩ **HIGH VIBE**

No matter how big or small . . .

Who is someone that has positively impacted my life and how?

_____

_____

_____

MY MANIFESTO

_____

_____

_____

_____

Today I have done the below to support my journey . . .

VISUALIZE ●   SELF-CARE ●   POSITIVE TALK ●

Today I need to let go of . . .

_____

_____

. . . to help me manifest.

I AM CAPABLE

What is my vibe like today?

Colour in how high vibe you are feeling today

LOW VIBE ⊂⎯⎯⎯⎯⎯⎯⎯⎯⎯⎯⎯⎯⎯⎯⎯⎯⎯⎯⎯⊃ **HIGH VIBE**

No matter how big or small . . .

What three things are bringing me joy right now and why?

_____

_____

_____

MY MANIFESTO

_____

_____

_____

Today I have done the below to support my journey . . .

VISUALIZE ●   SELF-CARE ●   POSITIVE TALK ●

Today I need to let go of . . .

_____

_____

. . . to help me manifest.

CLAIM IT

Positive affirmations are a powerful tool that can really help in your manifesting journey. Write out an affirmation for something you would like to attract in your life and repeat it below on each line.

_____

_____

_____

_____

_____

_____

_____

_____

_____

_____

_____

_____

_____

_____

_____

_____

_____

_____

Tip: Recite your affirmation out loud. What you verbalize, you materialize.

I AM AMBITIOUS

What is my vibe like today?

Colour in how high vibe you are feeling today

**LOW
VIBE** ⟨_____⟩ **HIGH
VIBE**

No matter how big or small . . .

Something positive I learned from a difficult situation is . . .

_____

_____

_____

MY MANIFESTO

_____

_____

_____

_____

Today I have done the below to support my journey . . .

VISUALIZE ⬤   SELF-CARE ⬤   POSITIVE TALK ⬤

Today I need to let go of . . .

_____

_____

. . . to help me manifest.

I AM COURAGEOUS

What is my vibe like today?

Colour in how high vibe you are feeling today

LOW VIBE (_____) **HIGH VIBE**

No matter how big or small . . .

Something that I am appreciative of every single day is . . .

_____

_____

_____

MY MANIFESTO

_____

_____

_____

_____

Today I have done the below to support my journey . . .

VISUALIZE ●   SELF-CARE ●   POSITIVE TALK ●

Today I need to let go of . . .

_____

_____

. . . to help me manifest.

I AM EMPOWERED

What is my vibe like today?

Colour in how high vibe you are feeling today

LOW VIBE ⬭ **HIGH VIBE**

No matter how big or small . . .

A time when I felt innovative was . . .

_____

_____

_____

MY MANIFESTO

_____

_____

_____

_____

Today I have done the below to support my journey . . .

VISUALIZE ⬤   SELF-CARE ⬤   POSITIVE TALK ⬤

Today I need to let go of . . .

_____

_____

. . . to help me manifest.

MY IDEAL LIFE

What does your ideal life look like? You can manifest your dream life by creating a comprehensive list of everything you desire. Be as detailed as you wish!

Tip: *Make sure you FEEL everything you write down.*

I AM MOTIVATED

What is my vibe like today?

Colour in how high vibe you are feeling today

LOW VIBE ⟨_____⟩ **HIGH VIBE**

No matter how big or small . . .

What challenge have I learned from and why?

_____

_____

_____

MY MANIFESTO

_____

_____

_____

_____

Today I have done the below to support my journey . . .

VISUALIZE ●   SELF-CARE ●   POSITIVE TALK ●

Today I need to let go of . . .

_____

_____

_____ . . . to help me manifest.

I AM STRONG

What is my vibe like today?

Colour in how high vibe you are feeling today

LOW VIBE ⬭ **HIGH VIBE**

No matter how big or small . . .

An opportunity I have received that has brought good things is . . .

_____

_____

_____

MY MANIFESTO

_____

_____

_____

Today I have done the below to support my journey . . .

VISUALIZE ⬤   SELF-CARE ⬤   POSITIVE TALK ⬤

Today I need to let go of . . .

_____

_____

. . . to help me manifest.

I AM FEARLESS

What is my vibe like today?

Colour in how high vibe you are feeling today

LOW VIBE ⟨_____⟩ **HIGH VIBE**

No matter how big or small . . .

Who is someone that loves and supports me unconditionally?

_____

_____

_____

MY MANIFESTO

_____

_____

_____

_____

Today I have done the below to support my journey . . .

VISUALIZE ●   SELF-CARE ●   POSITIVE TALK ●

Today I need to let go of . . .

_____

_____

. . . to help me manifest.

GRATITUDE CHALLENGE

 Get into a state of genuine appreciation with this fun gratitude challenge. Tick any of the below that you have managed to do recently. One box is left blank for you to fill in with something personal to you.

SAY THREE THINGS YOU ARE GRATEFUL FOR ABOUT YOURSELF

SPEND TEN MINUTES READING OR LISTENING TO SOMETHING THAT INSPIRES YOU

CALL A FRIEND TO CHECK UP ON THEM

DO SOMETHING ENJOYABLE WITH A LOVED ONE

LOOK IN THE MIRROR AND SEE HOW BEAUTIFUL YOU ARE

THANK SOMEONE FOR THEIR SERVICE

I AM DETERMINED

What is my vibe like today?

Colour in how high vibe you are feeling today

**LOW
VIBE** ⟨_____⟩ **HIGH
VIBE**

No matter how big or small . . .

What aspect of nature do I feel most thankful for?

_____

_____

_____

MY MANIFESTO

_____

_____

_____

_____

Today I have done the below to support my journey . . .

VISUALIZE ⬤   SELF-CARE ⬤   POSITIVE TALK ⬤

Today I need to let go of . . .

_____

_____

. . . to help me manifest.

I AM TENACIOUS

What is my vibe like today?

Colour in how high vibe you are feeling today

LOW VIBE ⟨_____⟩ **HIGH VIBE**

No matter how big or small . . .

What is one thing I have received recently that has brought me joy?

_____

_____

_____

MY MANIFESTO

_____

_____

_____

_____

Today I have done the below to support my journey . . .

VISUALIZE ⬤   SELF-CARE ⬤   POSITIVE TALK ⬤

Today I need to let go of . . .

_____

_____

. . . to help me manifest.

I AM PERSISTENT

What is my vibe like today?

Colour in how high vibe you are feeling today

LOW VIBE ⟨ _____ ⟩ **HIGH VIBE**

No matter how big or small...

A time when I felt both loved and appreciated was ...

_____

_____

_____

MY MANIFESTO

_____

_____

_____

_____

Today I have done the below to support my journey ...

VISUALIZE ●   SELF-CARE ●   POSITIVE TALK ●

Today I need to let go of ...

_____

_____

... to help me manifest.

AFFIRMATION COLOURING

 Colouring can be relaxing and satisfying. Let your creativity flow by colouring in this powerful affirmation and allow it to manifest.

I AM FOCUSED

What is my vibe like today?

Colour in how high vibe you are feeling today

LOW VIBE ⟨⎯⎯⎯⎯⎯⎯⎯⎯⎯⎯⎯⎯⎯⎯⎯⎯⎯⎯⟩ **HIGH VIBE**

No matter how big or small . . .

What is one little thing that happened today that had a big impact?

_____

_____

_____

MY MANIFESTO

_____

_____

_____

_____

Today I have done the below to support my journey . . .

VISUALIZE ●   **SELF-CARE** ●   **POSITIVE TALK** ●

Today I need to let go of . . .

_____

_____

. . . to help me manifest.

I AM DRIVEN

What is my vibe like today?

Colour in how high vibe you are feeling today

LOW VIBE ⟨_____⟩ **HIGH VIBE**

No matter how big or small . . .

What one thing do I appreciate about my body and its capabilities?

_____

_____

_____

MY MANIFESTO

_____

_____

_____

_____

Today I have done the below to support my journey . . .

VISUALIZE ●   SELF-CARE ●   POSITIVE TALK ●

Today I need to let go of . . .

_____

_____

. . . to help me manifest.

I AM INSPIRING

What is my vibe like today?

Colour in how high vibe you are feeling today

LOW VIBE ⟨ ⟩ **HIGH VIBE**

No matter how big or small . . .

A time I received validation for something I was unsure about was . . .

_____

_____

_____

MY MANIFESTO

_____

_____

_____

_____

Today I have done the below to support my journey . . .

VISUALIZE ●   SELF-CARE ●   POSITIVE TALK ●

Today I need to let go of . . .

_____

_____

. . . to help me manifest.

MANIFESTO MEMO

 Transform your manifesto into an audio format to serve as a daily prompt for all the things you aspire to achieve in life. You can effortlessly create an audio recording of your manifesto using your phone's memo or voice recorder app and listen to it regularly or whenever you require a reminder.

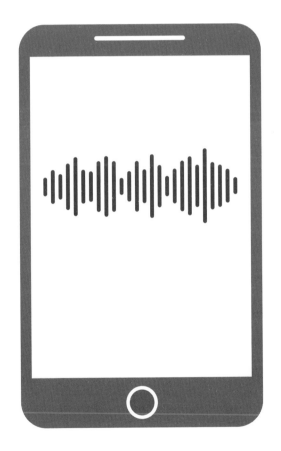

 Tip: You can also find this in your High Vibe Hacks Kit on page 8.

I AM RADIANT

What is my vibe like today?

Colour in how high vibe you are feeling today

LOW VIBE ⬭ **HIGH VIBE**

No matter how big or small . . .

A moment when I received unexpected kindness from someone was . . .

_____

_____

_____

MY MANIFESTO

_____

_____

_____

_____

Today I have done the below to support my journey . . .

VISUALIZE ⬤   SELF-CARE ⬤   POSITIVE TALK ⬤

Today I need to let go of . . .

_____

_____

. . . to help me manifest.

I AM UNSTOPPABLE

What is my vibe like today?

Colour in how high vibe you are feeling today

**LOW
VIBE** ⟨_____⟩ **HIGH
VIBE**

No matter how big or small . . .

What lesson has changed my life for the better and why?

_____

_____

_____

MY MANIFESTO

_____

_____

_____

_____

Today I have done the below to support my journey . . .

VISUALIZE ● SELF-CARE ● POSITIVE TALK ●

Today I need to let go of . . .

_____

_____

. . . to help me manifest.

I AM PASSIONATE

What is my vibe like today?

Colour in how high vibe you are feeling today

LOW VIBE ⟨　　　　　　　　　　　　　　　　　　　⟩ **HIGH VIBE**

No matter how big or small . . .

How has gratitude helped me cope with challenges?

_____

_____

_____

MY MANIFESTO

_____

_____

_____

_____

Today I have done the below to support my journey . . .

VISUALIZE ●　　　SELF-CARE ●　　　POSITIVE TALK ●

Today I need to let go of . . .

_____

_____

. . . to help me manifest.

A SPACE TO SCRIPT

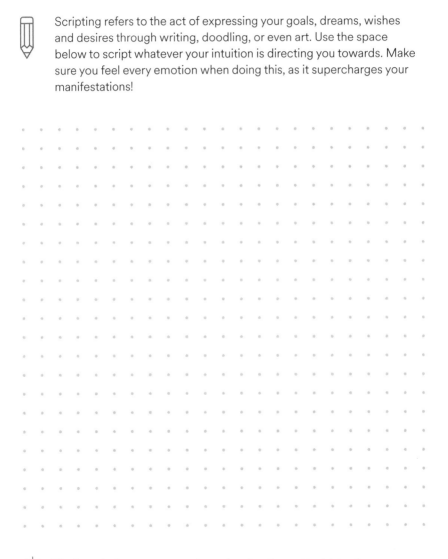

Scripting refers to the act of expressing your goals, dreams, wishes and desires through writing, doodling, or even art. Use the space below to script whatever your intuition is directing you towards. Make sure you feel every emotion when doing this, as it supercharges your manifestations!

Tip: Spend a few moments at the end to visualize and lock into place what you have scripted.

I AM DEDICATED

What is my vibe like today?

Colour in how high vibe you are feeling today

LOW VIBE ⟨_____⟩ **HIGH VIBE**

No matter how big or small . . .

A time when I felt truly connected to my body was . . .

_____

_____

_____

MY MANIFESTO

_____

_____

_____

_____

Today I have done the below to support my journey . . .

VISUALIZE ⬤   SELF-CARE ⬤   POSITIVE TALK ⬤

Today I need to let go of . . .

_____

_____

. . . to help me manifest.

I AM OPTIMISTIC

What is my vibe like today?

Colour in how high vibe you are feeling today

LOW VIBE ⟨ _____ ⟩ **HIGH VIBE**

No matter how big or small . . .

A time when I felt proud of myself for making a difficult decision was . . .

_____

_____

_____

MY MANIFESTO

_____

_____

_____

_____

Today I have done the below to support my journey . . .

VISUALIZE ⬤   SELF-CARE ⬤   POSITIVE TALK ⬤

Today I need to let go of . . .

_____

_____

. . . to help me manifest.

I AM FORTUNATE

What is my vibe like today?

Colour in how high vibe you are feeling today

**LOW
VIBE** ⬭ **HIGH
VIBE**

No matter how big or small . . .

What am I happy about in my current stage in life?

_____

_____

_____

MY MANIFESTO

_____

_____

_____

Today I have done the below to support my journey . . .

VISUALIZE ⬤   SELF-CARE ⬤   POSITIVE TALK ⬤

Today I need to let go of . . .

_____

_____

. . . to help me manifest.

FIVE SENSES TO MY DREAM LIFE

Begin by selecting one specific desire you wish to manifest and visualize it in great detail using all five of your senses. Imagine how it looks, feels, smells, tastes and sounds. Use the boxes below to write out the details. Dive deep into your emotions while doing this exercise. Let the sensory experience reinforce your ability to attract your desired outcome to you.

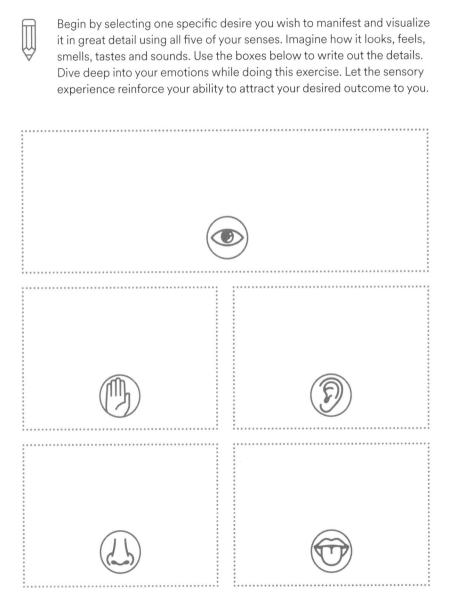

I AM CREATIVE

What is my vibe like today?

Colour in how high vibe you are feeling today

LOW VIBE ⟨_____⟩ **HIGH VIBE**

No matter how big or small . . .

A time when I made progress towards a goal was . . .

_____

_____

_____

MY MANIFESTO

_____

_____

_____

_____

Today I have done the below to support my journey . . .

VISUALIZE ●   SELF-CARE ●   POSITIVE TALK ●

Today I need to let go of . . .

_____

_____

. . . to help me manifest.

I AM RESOURCEFUL

What is my vibe like today?

Colour in how high vibe you are feeling today

LOW VIBE ⬭ **HIGH VIBE**

No matter how big or small . . .

What luxury am I grateful for and why?

_____

_____

_____

MY MANIFESTO

_____

_____

_____

_____

Today I have done the below to support my journey . . .

VISUALIZE ⬤   SELF-CARE ⬤   POSITIVE TALK ⬤

Today I need to let go of . . .

_____

_____

. . . to help me manifest.

I AM TALENTED

What is my vibe like today?

Colour in how high vibe you are feeling today

LOW VIBE ⟨ ⟩ **HIGH VIBE**

No matter how big or small . . .

A time I made a positive contribution towards something was . . .

_____

_____

_____

MY MANIFESTO

_____

_____

_____

_____

Today I have done the below to support my journey . . .

VISUALIZE ⬤   SELF-CARE ⬤   POSITIVE TALK ⬤

Today I need to let go of . . .

_____

_____

. . . to help me manifest.

MANIFEST PLAYLIST

Create a playlist with songs that help you raise your vibrations and get ready to attract everything you want in your life. Whenever you feel low in energy, come back to this playlist for a boost.

MANIFESTING MAGIC

1
2
3
4
5
6
7
8
9
10

 Tip: *Feeling stuck? Check out our playlist on Spotify!*

I AM INDEPENDENT

What is my vibe like today?

Colour in how high vibe you are feeling today

LOW VIBE ⬭──────────────────────────────⬭ **HIGH VIBE**

No matter how big or small . . .

What is something that has brought me a feeling of wonder recently?

_____

_____

_____

MY MANIFESTO

_____

_____

_____

Today I have done the below to support my journey . . .

VISUALIZE ●   SELF-CARE ●   POSITIVE TALK ●

Today I need to let go of . . .

_____

_____

. . . to help me manifest.

I AM WISE

What is my vibe like today?

Colour in how high vibe you are feeling today

**LOW
VIBE** ⊂⟶⟶⟶⟶⟶⟶⟶⟶⟶⟶⟶⟶⟶⟶⊃ **HIGH
VIBE**

No matter how big or small . . .

Who is someone that brings peace into my life and why?

_____

_____

_____

MY MANIFESTO

_____

_____

_____

_____

Today I have done the below to support my journey . . .

VISUALIZE ⬤   SELF-CARE ⬤   POSITIVE TALK ⬤

Today I need to let go of . . .

_____

_____

. . . to help me manifest.

I AM ADVENTUROUS

What is my vibe like today?

Colour in how high vibe you are feeling today

LOW VIBE ⬭ **HIGH VIBE**

No matter how big or small . . .

How do I express gratitude to others?

_____

_____

_____

MY MANIFESTO

_____

_____

_____

_____

Today I have done the below to support my journey . . .

VISUALIZE ⬤   SELF-CARE ⬤   POSITIVE TALK ⬤

Today I need to let go of . . .

_____

_____

. . . to help me manifest.

PILLOW METHOD

 The pillow manifestation method is an easy way to programme your subconscious mind to work towards manifesting your desires even while you sleep. Just follow these simple steps.

1. Decide what you want to manifest.

2. Grab a piece of paper and write down a powerful affirmation related to your desire.

3. Place the piece of paper under your pillow.

4. Every night before you fall asleep, visualize yourself already having achieved your goal. Imagine the details and feel the emotions associated with it while 'letting go' of any resistance that might be interfering with it.

5. Let the Universe take control and trust the process before you fall asleep with positive feelings and thoughts in your mind.

6. Continue this for 7–10 days, or until it feels right to remove the piece of paper.

I AM A VISIONARY

What is my vibe like today?

Colour in how high vibe you are feeling today

LOW
VIBE ⟨_____⟩ HIGH
VIBE

No matter how big or small . . .

A time when I felt confident in my abilities was . . .

_____

_____

_____

MY MANIFESTO

_____

_____

_____

_____

Today I have done the below to support my journey . . .

VISUALIZE ⬤   SELF-CARE ⬤   POSITIVE TALK ⬤

Today I need to let go of . . .

_____

_____

. . . to help me manifest.

I AM AUTHENTIC

What is my vibe like today?

Colour in how high vibe you are feeling today

LOW
VIBE

HIGH
VIBE

No matter how big or small . . .

What is one of the best things about being me and why?

_____

_____

_____

MY MANIFESTO

_____

_____

_____

_____

Today I have done the below to support my journey . . .

VISUALIZE ⬤   SELF-CARE ⬤   POSITIVE TALK ⬤

Today I need to let go of . . .

_____

_____

. . . to help me manifest.

I AM INNOVATIVE

What is my vibe like today?

Colour in how high vibe you are feeling today

**LOW
VIBE** ⟨_____⟩ **HIGH
VIBE**

No matter how big or small . . .

Who is someone that has contributed to my growth and how?

_____

_____

_____

MY MANIFESTO

_____

_____

_____

_____

Today I have done the below to support my journey . . .

VISUALIZE ⬤   SELF-CARE ⬤   POSITIVE TALK ⬤

Today I need to let go of . . .

_____

_____

. . . to help me manifest.

30-DAY MANIFEST CHECK-IN

Check in with how your manifestation journey is going and notice anything that needs to be tweaked to keep you on track.

WHAT WENT WELL OVER THE LAST 30 DAYS?

HOW AM I FEELING ABOUT MY MANIFESTING JOURNEY SO FAR?

IS THERE ANYTHING I STRUGGLED WITH?

IS THERE ANYTHING I COULD DO TO SUPPORT MY MANIFESTATIONS?

I AM COMPASSIONATE

What is my vibe like today?

Colour in how high vibe you are feeling today

LOW VIBE ⬭ **HIGH VIBE**

No matter how big or small . . .

A time I accomplished something I did not think was possible was . . .

_____

_____

_____

MY MANIFESTO

_____

_____

_____

_____

Today I have done the below to support my journey . . .

VISUALIZE ⬤   SELF-CARE ⬤   POSITIVE TALK ⬤

Today I need to let go of . . .

_____

_____

. . . to help me manifest.

I AM GRATEFUL

What is my vibe like today?

Colour in how high vibe you are feeling today

**LOW
VIBE** ⬭ **HIGH
VIBE**

No matter how big or small . . .

What is something I own that brings me joy?

_____

_____

_____

MY MANIFESTO

_____

_____

_____

_____

Today I have done the below to support my journey . . .

VISUALIZE ⬤   SELF-CARE ⬤   POSITIVE TALK ⬤

Today I need to let go of . . .

_____

_____

. . . to help me manifest.

I AM HUMBLE

What is my vibe like today?

Colour in how high vibe you are feeling today

LOW VIBE ⟨ ⟩ **HIGH VIBE**

No matter how big or small . . .

What is one thing that made me smile today and why?

_____

_____

_____

MY MANIFESTO

_____

_____

_____

_____

Today I have done the below to support my journey . . .

VISUALIZE ●   SELF-CARE ●   POSITIVE TALK ●

Today I need to let go of . . .

_____

_____

. . . to help me manifest.

CLAIM IT

Positive affirmations are a powerful tool that can really help in your manifesting journey. Write out an affirmation for something you would like to attract in your life and repeat it below on each line.

 Tip: Recite your affirmation out loud. What you verbalize, you materialize.

I AM TRUSTWORTHY

What is my vibe like today?

Colour in how high vibe you are feeling today

LOW VIBE ◯⟨⟩ **HIGH VIBE**

No matter how big or small . . .

What is something about myself I feel grateful for and why?

_____

_____

_____

MY MANIFESTO

_____

_____

_____

_____

Today I have done the below to support my journey . . .

VISUALIZE ⬤   SELF-CARE ⬤   POSITIVE TALK ⬤

Today I need to let go of . . .

_____

_____

. . . to help me manifest.

I AM GENEROUS

What is my vibe like today?

Colour in how high vibe you are feeling today

LOW VIBE ⊂⟩ **HIGH VIBE**

No matter how big or small . . .

What is one thing I accomplished today that I am proud of?

_____

_____

_____

MY MANIFESTO

_____

_____

_____

Today I have done the below to support my journey . . .

VISUALIZE ●   SELF-CARE ●   POSITIVE TALK ●

Today I need to let go of . . .

_____

_____

. . . to help me manifest.

I AM CARING

What is my vibe like today?

Colour in how high vibe you are feeling today

LOW VIBE (_____) **HIGH VIBE**

No matter how big or small . . .

What is one thing I am looking forward to in the future and why?

_____

_____

_____

MY MANIFESTO

_____

_____

_____

_____

Today I have done the below to support my journey . . .

VISUALIZE ⬤   SELF-CARE ⬤   POSITIVE TALK ⬤

Today I need to let go of . . .

_____

_____

. . . to help me manifest.

MY FUTURE SELF

It is time to meet your future self! In each box, describe what your future self has achieved. Believe in everything you write down and visualize it already happening. Let's go!

LIFE

_____
_____
_____
_____
_____
_____

CAREER

_____
_____
_____
_____
_____

LOVE

_____
_____
_____
_____
_____

FINANCE

_____
_____
_____
_____
_____

I AM EMPATHETIC

What is my vibe like today?

Colour in how high vibe you are feeling today

LOW VIBE ⬭ **HIGH VIBE**

No matter how big or small . . .

What is something I have in my life right now that I did not have a year ago?

_____

_____

_____

MY MANIFESTO

_____

_____

_____

Today I have done the below to support my journey . . .

VISUALIZE ● SELF-CARE ● POSITIVE TALK ●

Today I need to let go of . . .

_____

_____

. . . to help me manifest.

I AM THOUGHTFUL

What is my vibe like today?

Colour in how high vibe you are feeling today

LOW
VIBE

HIGH
VIBE

No matter how big or small . . .

What physical sensation do I enjoy and why?

_____

_____

_____

MY MANIFESTO

_____

_____

_____

_____

Today I have done the below to support my journey . . .

VISUALIZE ⬤   SELF-CARE ⬤   POSITIVE TALK ⬤

Today I need to let go of . . .

_____

_____

. . . to help me manifest.

I AM PATIENT

What is my vibe like today?

Colour in how high vibe you are feeling today

LOW VIBE (_____) **HIGH VIBE**

No matter how big or small . . .

A time when I received help and support was . . .

_____

_____

_____

MY MANIFESTO

_____

_____

_____

_____

Today I have done the below to support my journey . . .

VISUALIZE ●   SELF-CARE ●   POSITIVE TALK ●

Today I need to let go of . . .

_____

_____

. . . to help me manifest.

LOOKING OUT FOR GRATITUDE

Find the 11 hidden grateful, smiling faces in the image below, and let it be a reminder to look for things you are grateful for in your day-to-day life. By doing this, you will slowly train your mind to recognize all the good in your life.

I AM ADMIRED

What is my vibe like today?

Colour in how high vibe you are feeling today

LOW VIBE ⟨_____⟩ **HIGH VIBE**

No matter how big or small . . .

What is a positive change I have experienced in my life?

_____

_____

_____

MY MANIFESTO

_____

_____

_____

_____

Today I have done the below to support my journey . . .

VISUALIZE ⬤   SELF-CARE ⬤   POSITIVE TALK ⬤

Today I need to let go of . . .

_____

_____

. . . to help me manifest.

I AM CURIOUS

What is my vibe like today?

Colour in how high vibe you are feeling today

LOW
VIBE ⟨⎯⎯⎯⎯⎯⎯⎯⎯⎯⎯⎯⎯⎯⎯⎯⎯⎯⎯⎯⟩ HIGH
VIBE

No matter how big or small . . .

In this modern world, I feel lucky to have . . .

_____

_____

_____

MY MANIFESTO

_____

_____

_____

_____

Today I have done the below to support my journey . . .

VISUALIZE ● SELF-CARE ● POSITIVE TALK ●

Today I need to let go of . . .

_____

_____

. . . to help me manifest.

I AM WEALTHY

What is my vibe like today?

Colour in how high vibe you are feeling today

LOW VIBE ⟨ _____ ⟩ **HIGH VIBE**

No matter how big or small . . .

A time when I was in a state of pure joy and excitement was . . .

_____

_____

_____

MY MANIFESTO

_____

_____

_____

_____

Today I have done the below to support my journey . . .

VISUALIZE ⬤   SELF-CARE ⬤   POSITIVE TALK ⬤

Today I need to let go of . . .

_____

_____

. . . to help me manifest.

BANK OF UNIVERSAL ABUNDANCE

Activate prosperity with the abundance cheque – a powerful tool to help you align with the energy of limitless prosperity and visualize your intentions. Remember to hold firm to the belief that you are worthy of the wealth you seek and that it is already on its way to you.

BANK OF UNIVERSAL ABUNDANCE   11:11
888 Manifestation Bank
Mother Earth, Universe 11:11

PAY TO THE ORDER OF_____

AMOUNT_____

BANK OF UNIVERSAL ABUNDANCE
The Infinite Universe

FOR_____ SIGNATURE_____
77777777 5555555 11:11

Tip: You can also download a free cheque from www.therisingcircle.com and keep it in your wallet.

I AM INTELLIGENT

What is my vibe like today?

Colour in how high vibe you are feeling today

LOW VIBE ⟨_____⟩ **HIGH VIBE**

No matter how big or small . . .

When was a time I learned something valuable?

_____

_____

_____

MY MANIFESTO

_____

_____

_____

_____

Today I have done the below to support my journey . . .

VISUALIZE ●   SELF-CARE ●   POSITIVE TALK ●

Today I need to let go of . . .

_____

_____

. . . to help me manifest.

I AM ARTICULATE

What is my vibe like today?

Colour in how high vibe you are feeling today

LOW VIBE ⟨⎯⎯⎯⎯⎯⎯⎯⎯⎯⎯⎯⎯⎯⎯⎯⎯⎯⎯⎯⟩ **HIGH VIBE**

No matter how big or small . . .

A heartfelt compliment I recently received was . . .

_____

_____

_____

MY MANIFESTO

_____

_____

_____

_____

Today I have done the below to support my journey . . .

VISUALIZE ⬤   SELF-CARE ⬤   POSITIVE TALK ⬤

Today I need to let go of . . .

_____

_____

. . . to help me manifest.

I AM PERCEPTIVE

What is my vibe like today?

Colour in how high vibe you are feeling today

LOW VIBE ⟨_____⟩ **HIGH VIBE**

No matter how big or small . . .

What is one thing I am looking forward to next week and why?

_____

_____

_____

MY MANIFESTO

_____

_____

_____

_____

Today I have done the below to support my journey . . .

VISUALIZE ●   SELF-CARE ●   POSITIVE TALK ●

Today I need to let go of . . .

_____

_____

. . . to help me manifest.

MANIFEST CHALLENGE

 Challenge yourself and raise your vibration today. Tick any of the below that you have managed to do recently. One is left blank for you to fill in with something that is personal to you.

USE YOUR INTUITION TO DECIDE YOUR NEXT STEP

DO A FUN ACTIVITY TO RAISE YOUR VIBRATION

FOCUS ON ONE POSITIVE AFFIRMATION TODAY

DO ONE THING TO SUPPORT YOUR GOAL

RELEASE A LIMITING BELIEF

VISUALIZE A DESIRE YOU WANT TO MANIFEST

I AM VERSATILE

What is my vibe like today?

Colour in how high vibe you are feeling today

LOW VIBE ⟨_____⟩ **HIGH VIBE**

No matter how big or small . . .

What talent or skill do I have that I am proud of?

_____

_____

_____

MY MANIFESTO

_____

_____

_____

_____

Today I have done the below to support my journey . . .

VISUALIZE ⚫   SELF-CARE ⚫   POSITIVE TALK ⚫

Today I need to let go of . . .

_____

_____

. . . to help me manifest.

I AM ONE OF A KIND

What is my vibe like today?

Colour in how high vibe you are feeling today

**LOW
VIBE** ⬭ **HIGH
VIBE**

No matter how big or small . . .

What is a moment that made me feel fulfilled?

_____

_____

_____

MY MANIFESTO

_____

_____

_____

_____

Today I have done the below to support my journey . . .

VISUALIZE ⬤   SELF-CARE ⬤   POSITIVE TALK ⬤

Today I need to let go of . . .

_____

_____

. . . to help me manifest.

_____

I AM INFLUENTIAL

What is my vibe like today?

Colour in how high vibe you are feeling today

LOW VIBE (_____) **HIGH VIBE**

No matter how big or small . . .

A time I really felt adored was . . .

_____

_____

_____

MY MANIFESTO

_____

_____

_____

_____

Today I have done the below to support my journey . . .

VISUALIZE ⬤   SELF-CARE ⬤   POSITIVE TALK ⬤

Today I need to let go of . . .

_____

_____

. . . to help me manifest.

A SPACE TO SCRIPT

Scripting refers to the act of expressing your goals, dreams, wishes and desires through writing, doodling or even art. Use the space below to script whatever your intuition is directing you towards. Make sure you feel every emotion when doing this, as it supercharges your manifestations!

Tip: *Spend a few moments at the end to visualize and lock into place what you have scripted.*

I AM CHARISMATIC

What is my vibe like today?

Colour in how high vibe you are feeling today

**LOW
VIBE** ⬭⬭⬭⬭⬭⬭⬭⬭⬭⬭⬭⬭⬭ **HIGH
VIBE**

No matter how big or small . . .

What is one of the greatest things about being me?

_____

_____

_____

MY MANIFESTO

_____

_____

_____

_____

Today I have done the below to support my journey . . .

VISUALIZE ⬤   SELF-CARE ⬤   POSITIVE TALK ⬤

Today I need to let go of . . .

_____

_____

. . . to help me manifest.

I AM POSITIVE

What is my vibe like today?

Colour in how high vibe you are feeling today

LOW VIBE ⟨ _____ ⟩ **HIGH VIBE**

No matter how big or small . . .

What do I love about my life and why?

_____

_____

_____

MY MANIFESTO

_____

_____

_____

_____

Today I have done the below to support my journey . . .

VISUALIZE ⬤   SELF-CARE ⬤   POSITIVE TALK ⬤

Today I need to let go of . . .

_____

_____

. . . to help me manifest.

I AM JOYFUL

What is my vibe like today?

Colour in how high vibe you are feeling today

LOW VIBE ⟨ ⟩ **HIGH VIBE**

No matter how big or small . . .

When did I last make time for myself and can I do this more often?

_____

_____

_____

MY MANIFESTO

_____

_____

_____

_____

Today I have done the below to support my journey . . .

VISUALIZE ⬤   SELF-CARE ⬤   POSITIVE TALK ⬤

Today I need to let go of . . .

_____

_____

. . . to help me manifest.

THOUGHT SWAP

What we think about, we bring about. Our thoughts dictate our life and how we handle different situations. Negative thoughts can hold us back and prevent our manifestations from unfolding. Let us change these negative thoughts to positive ones by replacing them.

1

2

3

I AM HAPPY

What is my vibe like today?

Colour in how high vibe you are feeling today

LOW VIBE ⟨_____⟩ **HIGH VIBE**

No matter how big or small . . .

I can be gentle to myself by . . .

_____

_____

_____

MY MANIFESTO

_____

_____

_____

_____

Today I have done the below to support my journey . . .

VISUALIZE ●   SELF-CARE ●   POSITIVE TALK ●

Today I need to let go of . . .

_____

_____

. . . to help me manifest.

I AM GRACIOUS

What is my vibe like today?

Colour in how high vibe you are feeling today

LOW VIBE ⊂⎯⎯⎯⎯⎯⎯⎯⎯⎯⎯⎯⎯⎯⎯⎯⎯⎯⎯⎯⊃ **HIGH VIBE**

No matter how big or small . . .

What is a personal quality that I appreciate about myself?

_____

_____

_____

MY MANIFESTO

_____

_____

_____

_____

Today I have done the below to support my journey . . .

VISUALIZE ●   SELF-CARE ●   POSITIVE TALK ●

Today I need to let go of . . .

_____

_____

. . . to help me manifest.

I AM FORGIVING

What is my vibe like today?

Colour in how high vibe you are feeling today

**LOW
VIBE** ⟨⟩ **HIGH
VIBE**

No matter how big or small . . .

Something that I hope to never forget is . . .

_____

_____

_____

MY MANIFESTO

_____

_____

_____

_____

Today I have done the below to support my journey . . .

VISUALIZE ⬤   SELF-CARE ⬤   POSITIVE TALK ⬤

Today I need to let go of . . .

_____

_____

. . . to help me manifest.

HIGH VIBE INSPO

 Think about all the wonderful things that inspire you and raise your vibes. Write them down and come back to them whenever you need a pick-me-up.

PODCASTS

SONGS

BOOKS

MOVIES

ROLE MODELS

LOVED ONES

 Tip: Add your inspiration list to your 'High Vibes Hacks Kit' on page 9.

I AM NURTURING

What is my vibe like today?

Colour in how high vibe you are feeling today

LOW VIBE $\longleftarrow$ ( ) $\longrightarrow$ **HIGH VIBE**

No matter how big or small . . .

What is a kind gesture that someone has done for me recently?

_____

_____

_____

MY MANIFESTO

_____

_____

_____

_____

Today I have done the below to support my journey . . .

VISUALIZE ⬤   SELF-CARE ⬤   POSITIVE TALK ⬤

Today I need to let go of . . .

_____

_____

. . . to help me manifest.

I AM PROUD

What is my vibe like today?

Colour in how high vibe you are feeling today

**LOW
VIBE** ⊂_____⊃ **HIGH
VIBE**

No matter how big or small . . .

What is something in my daily routine that brings me serenity and why?

_____

_____

_____

MY MANIFESTO

_____

_____

_____

_____

Today I have done the below to support my journey . . .

VISUALIZE ●   SELF-CARE ●   POSITIVE TALK ●

Today I need to let go of . . .

_____

_____

. . . to help me manifest.

I AM PLAYFUL

What is my vibe like today?

Colour in how high vibe you are feeling today

**LOW
VIBE** ⟨_____⟩ **HIGH
VIBE**

No matter how big or small...

A space I feel grateful to have is...

_____

_____

_____

MY MANIFESTO

_____

_____

_____

_____

Today I have done the below to support my journey...

VISUALIZE ⬤   SELF-CARE ⬤   POSITIVE TALK ⬤

Today I need to let go of...

_____

_____

... to help me manifest.

WOOP METHOD

 WOOP, popularized by Gabriele Oettingen, is a four-step goal-setting method that helps you turn wishful thinking into reality. Simply fill out the boxes below.

WISH

Identify your goal or desire. Be specific about what you want.

OUTCOME

Think about the best possible outcome for achieving your goal.

OBSTACLE

Identify any challenges that may stand in the way of achieving your goal.

PLAN

Write down the specific action steps you will take to overcome the obstacle and achieve your goal.

I AM HONEST

What is my vibe like today?

Colour in how high vibe you are feeling today

**LOW
VIBE** ⟨_____⟩ **HIGH
VIBE**

No matter how big or small . . .

A moment of kindness I showed to someone was . . .

_____

_____

_____

MY MANIFESTO

_____

_____

_____

_____

Today I have done the below to support my journey . . .

VISUALIZE ⬤   SELF-CARE ⬤   POSITIVE TALK ⬤

Today I need to let go of . . .

_____

_____

. . . to help me manifest.

I AM LOYAL

What is my vibe like today?

Colour in how high vibe you are feeling today

LOW VIBE ⟨_____⟩ **HIGH VIBE**

No matter how big or small . . .

A book or an article that influenced me positively is . . .

_____

_____

_____

MY MANIFESTO

_____

_____

_____

_____

Today I have done the below to support my journey . . .

VISUALIZE ⬤   SELF-CARE ⬤   POSITIVE TALK ⬤

Today I need to let go of . . .

_____

_____

. . . to help me manifest.

I AM RISING

What is my vibe like today?

Colour in how high vibe you are feeling today

LOW VIBE ⟨_____⟩ **HIGH VIBE**

No matter how big or small . . .

A learning that I have benefited from is . . .

_____

_____

_____

MY MANIFESTO

_____

_____

_____

_____

Today I have done the below to support my journey . . .

VISUALIZE ⬤   SELF-CARE ⬤   POSITIVE TALK ⬤

Today I need to let go of . . .

_____

_____

. . . to help me manifest.

30-DAY MANIFEST CHECK-IN

Check in with how your manifestation journey is going and notice anything that needs to be tweaked to keep you on track.

WHAT WENT WELL OVER THE LAST 30 DAYS?

HOW AM I FEELING ABOUT MY MANIFESTING JOURNEY SO FAR?

IS THERE ANYTHING I STRUGGLED WITH?

IS THERE ANYTHING I COULD DO TO SUPPORT MY MANIFESTATIONS?

I AM BALANCED

What is my vibe like today?

Colour in how high vibe you are feeling today

LOW VIBE ⊂_____⊃ **HIGH VIBE**

No matter how big or small . . .

Who is someone I shared a beautiful experience with recently?

_____

_____

_____

MY MANIFESTO

_____

_____

_____

_____

Today I have done the below to support my journey . . .

VISUALIZE ⬤   SELF-CARE ⬤   POSITIVE TALK ⬤

Today I need to let go of . . .

_____

_____

. . . to help me manifest.

I AM UPLIFTED

What is my vibe like today?

Colour in how high vibe you are feeling today

**LOW
VIBE** ⊂⟨_____⟩⊃ **HIGH
VIBE**

No matter how big or small . . .

Something I have been putting off that I have finally done was . . .

_____

_____

_____

MY MANIFESTO

_____

_____

_____

_____

Today I have done the below to support my journey . . .

VISUALIZE ●   SELF-CARE ●   POSITIVE TALK ●

Today I need to let go of . . .

_____

_____

. . . to help me manifest.

I AM DEVOTED

What is my vibe like today?

Colour in how high vibe you are feeling today

**LOW
VIBE** ⟨_____⟩ **HIGH
VIBE**

No matter how big or small . . .

The place that inspires me the most is . . .

_____

_____

_____

MY MANIFESTO

_____

_____

_____

_____

Today I have done the below to support my journey . . .

VISUALIZE ⬤   SELF-CARE ⬤   POSITIVE TALK ⬤

Today I need to let go of . . .

_____

_____

. . . to help me manifest.

CLAIM IT

Positive affirmations are a powerful tool that can really help in your manifesting journey. Write out an affirmation for something you would like to attract in your life and repeat it below on each line.

_____

_____

_____

_____

_____

_____

_____

_____

_____

_____

_____

_____

_____

_____

_____

_____

_____

_____

 Tip: _Recite your affirmation out loud. What you verbalize, you materialize._

I AM THANKFUL

What is my vibe like today?

Colour in how high vibe you are feeling today

LOW VIBE ⟨_____⟩ **HIGH VIBE**

No matter how big or small . . .

An item I use every day that I am grateful for is . . .

_____

_____

_____

MY MANIFESTO

_____

_____

_____

_____

Today I have done the below to support my journey . . .

VISUALIZE ⬤   SELF-CARE ⬤   POSITIVE TALK ⬤

Today I need to let go of . . .

_____

_____

. . . to help me manifest.

I AM FREE

What is my vibe like today?

Colour in how high vibe you are feeling today

LOW VIBE   ⊂_____⊃   **HIGH VIBE**

No matter how big or small . . .

A self-care act that brings me joy is . . .

_____

_____

_____

MY MANIFESTO

_____

_____

_____

_____

Today I have done the below to support my journey . . .

VISUALIZE ⬤   SELF-CARE ⬤   POSITIVE TALK ⬤

Today I need to let go of . . .

_____

_____

. . . to help me manifest.

I AM GROUNDED

What is my vibe like today?

Colour in how high vibe you are feeling today

LOW VIBE ⬭ **HIGH VIBE**

No matter how big or small . . .

I feel connected to the Universe when . . .

_____

_____

_____

MY MANIFESTO

_____

_____

_____

_____

Today I have done the below to support my journey . . .

VISUALIZE ⬤   SELF-CARE ⬤   POSITIVE TALK ⬤

Today I need to let go of . . .

_____

_____

. . . to help me manifest.

I'M SO BLESSED

The Universe is ready to bless you with all that you desire. Ask and you shall receive. What blessings are you going to request? Write below a blessing you wish you had and imagine it is already yours, e.g. 'I absolutely love my new job as a teacher.'

I'M SO BLESSED . . .

I'M SO BLESSED . . .

I'M SO BLESSED . . .

I'M SO BLESSED . . .

I'M SO BLESSED . . .

I AM HEALTHY

What is my vibe like today?

Colour in how high vibe you are feeling today

LOW VIBE ⟨ ⟩ **HIGH VIBE**

No matter how big or small . . .

An area in my life where I feel truly content is . . .

_____

_____

_____

MY MANIFESTO

_____

_____

_____

Today I have done the below to support my journey . . .

VISUALIZE ●   SELF-CARE ●   POSITIVE TALK ●

Today I need to let go of . . .

_____

_____

. . . to help me manifest.

I AM WHOLE

What is my vibe like today?

Colour in how high vibe you are feeling today

LOW
VIBE ⬭ HIGH
VIBE

No matter how big or small . . .

Someone that has shown me love is . . .

_____

_____

_____

MY MANIFESTO

_____

_____

_____

_____

Today I have done the below to support my journey . . .

VISUALIZE ⬤   SELF-CARE ⬤   POSITIVE TALK ⬤

Today I need to let go of . . .

_____

_____

. . . to help me manifest.

I AM CONNECTED

What is my vibe like today?

Colour in how high vibe you are feeling today

LOW VIBE ⟨⎯⎯⎯⎯⎯⎯⎯⎯⎯⎯⎯⎯⎯⎯⎯⟩ **HIGH VIBE**

No matter how big or small . . .

A place that holds a special meaning to me is . . .

_____

_____

_____

MY MANIFESTO

_____

_____

_____

Today I have done the below to support my journey . . .

VISUALIZE ● SELF-CARE ● POSITIVE TALK ●

Today I need to let go of . . .

_____

_____

. . . to help me manifest.

MY MAGIC BOX

 Your manifestation box is ready for your intentions and objects to place in it. Jot down anything that resonates with your desired outcome, infuse it with positive energy, and call out to the Universe. Refer to the box regularly to vividly picture your intention materializing in your life.

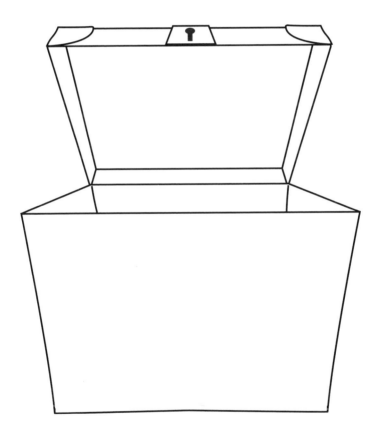

 Tip: *Next time you have an empty box, make it into a physical manifestation box!*

I AM ABUNDANT

What is my vibe like today?

Colour in how high vibe you are feeling today

LOW VIBE ⟨_____⟩ **HIGH VIBE**

No matter how big or small . . .

What is one reason to smile and why?

_____

_____

_____

MY MANIFESTO

_____

_____

_____

_____

Today I have done the below to support my journey . . .

VISUALIZE ⬤   SELF-CARE ⬤   POSITIVE TALK ⬤

Today I need to let go of . . .

_____

_____

. . . to help me manifest.

I AM WORTHY

What is my vibe like today?

Colour in how high vibe you are feeling today

LOW
VIBE
HIGH
VIBE

No matter how big or small . . .

A wisdom that I gained is . . .

_____

_____

_____

MY MANIFESTO

_____

_____

_____

Today I have done the below to support my journey . . .

VISUALIZE ⬤   SELF-CARE ⬤   POSITIVE TALK ⬤

Today I need to let go of . . .

_____

_____

. . . to help me manifest.

I AM VALUABLE

What is my vibe like today?

Colour in how high vibe you are feeling today

LOW VIBE ⟨_____⟩ **HIGH VIBE**

No matter how big or small . . .

What is one constant in my life that makes me feel good?

_____

_____

_____

MY MANIFESTO

_____

_____

_____

_____

Today I have done the below to support my journey . . .

VISUALIZE ⬤   SELF-CARE ⬤   POSITIVE TALK ⬤

Today I need to let go of . . .

_____

_____

. . . to help me manifest.

ORDERING FROM THE UNIVERSE

Express your desires to the Universe with clarity and precision. There are no limits to what you can request, so ask for all that your heart desires. Have faith in your requests, release any doubts, and embrace with gratitude the abundance that is rightfully yours.

DEAR UNIVERSE

ORDER #1111

ORDER DATE _____

CUSTOMER NAME _____

DESIRE NO #	DESCRIPTION	TOTAL
		FREE
		FREE
		FREE
		FREE
		FREE
		FREE
		FREE
		FREE

Your blessings are on their way!

I AM EXCITED

What is my vibe like today?

Colour in how high vibe you are feeling today

**LOW
VIBE** (_____) **HIGH
VIBE**

No matter how big or small . . .

What is a small moment that brings me a lot of happiness?

_____

_____

_____

MY MANIFESTO

_____

_____

_____

_____

Today I have done the below to support my journey . . .

VISUALIZE ⬤   SELF-CARE ⬤   POSITIVE TALK ⬤

Today I need to let go of . . .

_____

_____

. . . to help me manifest.

I AM NOURISHED

What is my vibe like today?

Colour in how high vibe you are feeling today

LOW VIBE ⬭ **HIGH VIBE**

No matter how big or small . . .

A personal trait I would never change about myself is . . .

_____

_____

_____

MY MANIFESTO

_____

_____

_____

_____

Today I have done the below to support my journey . . .

VISUALIZE ⬤   SELF-CARE ⬤   POSITIVE TALK ⬤

Today I need to let go of . . .

_____

_____

. . . to help me manifest.

I AM CALM

What is my vibe like today?

Colour in how high vibe you are feeling today

LOW VIBE ⟨ ⟩ **HIGH VIBE**

No matter how big or small . . .

A time when I truly believed in myself was . . .

_____

_____

_____

MY MANIFESTO

_____

_____

_____

_____

Today I have done the below to support my journey . . .

VISUALIZE ●   SELF-CARE ●   POSITIVE TALK ●

Today I need to let go of . . .

_____

_____

. . . to help me manifest.

DOT-TO-DOT

Join the dots to reveal a powerful message just for you.

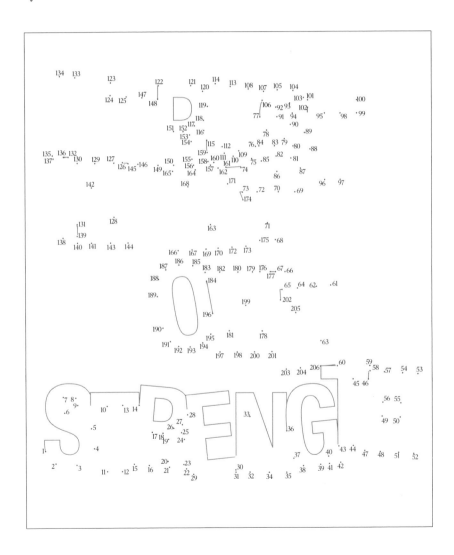

I AM OPEN-MINDED

What is my vibe like today?

Colour in how high vibe you are feeling today

LOW VIBE ⟨_____⟩ **HIGH VIBE**

No matter how big or small . . .

An act of kindness I recently witnessed was . . .

_____

_____

_____

MY MANIFESTO

_____

_____

_____

_____

Today I have done the below to support my journey . . .

VISUALIZE ⬤   SELF-CARE ⬤   POSITIVE TALK ⬤

Today I need to let go of . . .

_____

_____

. . . to help me manifest.

I AM REFRESHED

What is my vibe like today?

Colour in how high vibe you are feeling today

LOW VIBE ( ) **HIGH VIBE**

No matter how big or small . . .

Someone I can have an honest conversation with is . . .

_____

_____

_____

MY MANIFESTO

_____

_____

_____

_____

Today I have done the below to support my journey . . .

VISUALIZE 　　　SELF-CARE 　　　POSITIVE TALK

Today I need to let go of . . .

_____

_____

. . . to help me manifest.

I AM A MAGNET

What is my vibe like today?

Colour in how high vibe you are feeling today

LOW VIBE ⟨_____⟩ **HIGH VIBE**

No matter how big or small . . .

A place that contributes to my well-being is . . .

_____

_____

_____

MY MANIFESTO

_____

_____

_____

_____

Today I have done the below to support my journey . . .

VISUALIZE ⬤   SELF-CARE ⬤   POSITIVE TALK ⬤

Today I need to let go of . . .

_____

_____

. . . to help me manifest.

A SPACE TO SCRIPT

Scripting refers to the act of expressing your goals, dreams, wishes and desires through writing, doodling, or even art. Use the space below to script whatever your intuition is directing you towards. Make sure you feel every emotion when doing this, as it supercharges your manifestations!

 Tip: *Spend a few moments at the end to visualize and lock into place what you have scripted.*

I AM BLESSED

What is my vibe like today?

Colour in how high vibe you are feeling today

LOW VIBE (⸏⸏⸏⸏⸏⸏⸏⸏⸏⸏⸏⸏⸏⸏⸏⸏⸏⸏⸏) **HIGH VIBE**

No matter how big or small . . .

Someone that inspired me to pursue my dreams is . . .

_____

_____

_____

MY MANIFESTO

_____

_____

_____

_____

Today I have done the below to support my journey . . .

VISUALIZE ●   SELF-CARE ●   POSITIVE TALK ●

Today I need to let go of . . .

_____

_____

. . . to help me manifest.

I AM LIMITLESS

What is my vibe like today?

Colour in how high vibe you are feeling today

LOW
VIBE

HIGH
VIBE

No matter how big or small . . .

A moment of kindness that impacted my day was . . .

MY MANIFESTO

Today I have done the below to support my journey . . .

VISUALIZE ⬤   SELF-CARE ⬤   POSITIVE TALK ⬤

Today I need to let go of . . .

. . . to help me manifest.

I AM RELEASING

What is my vibe like today?

Colour in how high vibe you are feeling today

LOW VIBE ⟨_____⟩ **HIGH VIBE**

No matter how big or small . . .

A physical ability I am grateful for is . . .

_____

_____

_____

MY MANIFESTO

_____

_____

_____

_____

Today I have done the below to support my journey . . .

VISUALIZE ⬤   SELF-CARE ⬤   POSITIVE TALK ⬤

Today I need to let go of . . .

_____

_____

. . . to help me manifest.

I AM

Empower yourself by crafting your own affirmations and writing them in the bubbles. Make it a habit to regularly revisit them and confidently say them aloud with pride!

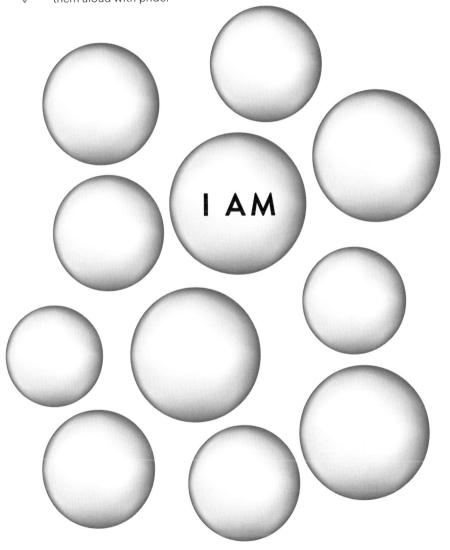

I AM

I AM WELCOMING

What is my vibe like today?

Colour in how high vibe you are feeling today

LOW
VIBE
HIGH
VIBE

No matter how big or small . . .

A time when I felt proud of someone else's accomplishment was . . .

_____

_____

MY MANIFESTO

_____

_____

_____

Today I have done the below to support my journey . . .

VISUALIZE ● SELF-CARE ● POSITIVE TALK ●

Today I need to let go of . . .

_____

_____

. . . to help me manifest.

I AM ACCEPTING

What is my vibe like today?

Colour in how high vibe you are feeling today

LOW VIBE ⟨_____⟩ **HIGH VIBE**

No matter how big or small . . .

A time when I was able to help someone in need was . . .

_____

_____

_____

MY MANIFESTO

_____

_____

_____

_____

Today I have done the below to support my journey . . .

VISUALIZE ⬤   SELF-CARE ⬤   POSITIVE TALK ⬤

Today I need to let go of . . .

_____

_____

. . . to help me manifest.

I AM BLOOMING

What is my vibe like today?

Colour in how high vibe you are feeling today

**LOW
VIBE** (_____) **HIGH
VIBE**

No matter how big or small . . .

A future goal I am excited to pursue is . . .

_____

_____

_____

MY MANIFESTO

_____

_____

_____

_____

Today I have done the below to support my journey . . .

VISUALIZE ⬤   SELF-CARE ⬤   POSITIVE TALK ⬤

Today I need to let go of . . .

_____

_____

. . . to help me manifest.

FROM ME TO THE UNIVERSE

Trust that the Universe is always working in your favour. For this, you have to be clear with what you are going to do and what you are going to leave to the Universe to do for you. Fill out the list below and be precise.

WHAT I AM DOING FOR ME TODAY	WHAT THE UNIVERSE IS DOING FOR ME

I AM CONTENT

What is my vibe like today?

Colour in how high vibe you are feeling today

LOW VIBE ⟨_____⟩ **HIGH VIBE**

No matter how big or small . . .

What makes me cheerful?

_____

_____

_____

MY MANIFESTO

_____

_____

_____

_____

Today I have done the below to support my journey . . .

VISUALIZE ⬤   SELF-CARE ⬤   POSITIVE TALK ⬤

Today I need to let go of . . .

_____

_____

. . . to help me manifest.

I AM GREAT

What is my vibe like today?

Colour in how high vibe you are feeling today

LOW
VIBE
HIGH
VIBE

No matter how big or small . . .

What brings me a sense of calm when I need it the most?

_____

_____

_____

MY MANIFESTO

_____

_____

_____

_____

Today I have done the below to support my journey . . .

VISUALIZE ⬤   SELF-CARE ⬤   POSITIVE TALK ⬤

Today I need to let go of . . .

_____

_____

. . . to help me manifest.

I AM SECURE

What is my vibe like today?

Colour in how high vibe you are feeling today

LOW VIBE ⬭──────────────────────────────⬭ **HIGH VIBE**

No matter how big or small . . .

A song that lifts my mood is . . .

_____

_____

_____

MY MANIFESTO

_____

_____

_____

_____

Today I have done the below to support my journey . . .

VISUALIZE ⚪   SELF-CARE ⚪   POSITIVE TALK ⚪

Today I need to let go of . . .

_____

_____

. . . to help me manifest.

AFFIRMATION COLOURING

Colouring can be relaxing and satisfying. Let your creativity flow by colouring in this powerful affirmation and allow it to manifest.

I AM FULFILLED

What is my vibe like today?

Colour in how high vibe you are feeling today

LOW
VIBE (_____) HIGH
VIBE

No matter how big or small . . .

A time when the Universe bought me an unexpected blessing was . . .

_____

_____

_____

MY MANIFESTO

_____

_____

_____

_____

Today I have done the below to support my journey . . .

VISUALIZE ⬤   SELF-CARE ⬤   POSITIVE TALK ⬤

Today I need to let go of . . .

_____

_____

. . . to help me manifest.

I AM GIFTED

What is my vibe like today?

Colour in how high vibe you are feeling today

**LOW
VIBE** (_____) **HIGH
VIBE**

No matter how big or small . . .

A moment when I felt a sense of empowerment was . . .

_____

_____

_____

MY MANIFESTO

_____

_____

_____

_____

Today I have done the below to support my journey . . .

VISUALIZE ⬤   SELF-CARE ⬤   POSITIVE TALK ⬤

Today I need to let go of . . .

_____

_____

. . . to help me manifest.

I AM SAFE

What is my vibe like today?

Colour in how high vibe you are feeling today

LOW VIBE ⟮_____⟯ **HIGH VIBE**

No matter how big or small . . .

A healing I will always appreciate is . . .

_____

_____

_____

MY MANIFESTO

_____

_____

_____

_____

Today I have done the below to support my journey . . .

VISUALIZE ⬤   SELF-CARE ⬤   POSITIVE TALK ⬤

Today I need to let go of . . .

_____

_____

. . . to help me manifest.

30-DAY MANIFEST CHECK-IN

Check in with how your manifestation journey is going and notice anything that needs to be tweaked to keep you on track.

WHAT WENT WELL OVER THE LAST 30 DAYS?

HOW AM I FEELING ABOUT MY MANIFESTING JOURNEY SO FAR?

IS THERE ANYTHING I STRUGGLED WITH?

IS THERE ANYTHING I COULD DO TO SUPPORT MY MANIFESTATIONS?

I AM LIBERATED

What is my vibe like today?

Colour in how high vibe you are feeling today

LOW VIBE ⟨_____⟩ **HIGH VIBE**

No matter how big or small . . .

A bond that I will always cherish is . . .

_____

_____

_____

MY MANIFESTO

_____

_____

_____

_____

Today I have done the below to support my journey . . .

VISUALIZE ⬤   SELF-CARE ⬤   POSITIVE TALK ⬤

Today I need to let go of . . .

_____

_____

. . . to help me manifest.

I AM LOVED

What is my vibe like today?

Colour in how high vibe you are feeling today

LOW VIBE ⟨⎯⎯⎯⎯⎯⎯⎯⎯⎯⎯⎯⎯⎯⎯⎯⎯⎯⟩ **HIGH VIBE**

No matter how big or small . . .

Someone that influences my values is . . .

_____

_____

_____

MY MANIFESTO

_____

_____

_____

_____

Today I have done the below to support my journey . . .

VISUALIZE ⬤   SELF-CARE ⬤   POSITIVE TALK ⬤

Today I need to let go of . . .

_____

_____

. . . to help me manifest.

I AM MINDFUL

What is my vibe like today?

Colour in how high vibe you are feeling today

**LOW
VIBE** ⟨ ⟩ **HIGH
VIBE**

No matter how big or small . . .

Who or what brings me a sense of purpose and fulfilment?

_____

_____

_____

MY MANIFESTO

_____

_____

_____

_____

Today I have done the below to support my journey . . .

VISUALIZE ●   SELF-CARE ●   POSITIVE TALK ●

Today I need to let go of . . .

_____

_____

. . . to help me manifest.

CLAIM IT

Positive affirmations are a powerful tool that can really help in your manifesting journey. Write out an affirmation for something you would like to attract in your life and repeat it below on each line.

_____

_____

_____

_____

_____

_____

_____

_____

_____

_____

_____

_____

_____

_____

_____

_____

_____

Tip: *Recite your affirmation out loud. What you verbalize, you materialize.*

I AM PRESENT

What is my vibe like today?

Colour in how high vibe you are feeling today

LOW
VIBE ⟨───────────────────────────────⟩ HIGH
VIBE

No matter how big or small . . .

An experience that allowed me to move forward with positivity was . . .

_____

_____

_____

MY MANIFESTO

_____

_____

_____

_____

Today I have done the below to support my journey . . .

VISUALIZE ⬤   SELF-CARE ⬤   POSITIVE TALK ⬤

Today I need to let go of . . .

_____

_____

. . . to help me manifest.

i AM LUCKY

What is my vibe like today?

Colour in how high vibe you are feeling today

LOW VIBE ⊂_____⊃ **HIGH VIBE**

No matter how big or small . . .

A moment of joy I shared with someone recently was . . .

_____

_____

_____

MY MANIFESTO

_____

_____

_____

_____

Today I have done the below to support my journey . . .

VISUALIZE ⬤   SELF-CARE ⬤   POSITIVE TALK ⬤

Today I need to let go of . . .

_____

_____

. . . to help me manifest.

I AM HOPEFUL

What is my vibe like today?

Colour in how high vibe you are feeling today

LOW
VIBE
⟨ ⟩
HIGH
VIBE

No matter how big or small . . .

A time when I overcame a limiting belief was . . .

_____

_____

_____

MY MANIFESTO

_____

_____

_____

Today I have done the below to support my journey . . .

VISUALIZE ⬤   SELF-CARE ⬤   POSITIVE TALK ⬤

Today I need to let go of . . .

_____

_____

. . . to help me manifest.

LETTER FROM MY FUTURE SELF

 Envision your future self and desired lifestyle in great detail by putting it down on paper. Include every little aspect of where you want to be and how it makes you feel. For example, you might write, 'I am thrilled to be living in my dream home!' Remember to be specific and maintain a positive attitude, allowing the manifestation process to unfold naturally.

Dear

I AM EVOLVING

What is my vibe like today?

Colour in how high vibe you are feeling today

LOW VIBE ⟨ _____ ⟩ **HIGH VIBE**

No matter how big or small . . .

One thing I am grateful for about my health is . . .

_____

_____

_____

MY MANIFESTO

_____

_____

_____

_____

Today I have done the below to support my journey . . .

VISUALIZE ●   SELF-CARE ●   POSITIVE TALK ●

Today I need to let go of . . .

_____

_____

. . . to help me manifest.

I AM COMMITTED

What is my vibe like today?

Colour in how high vibe you are feeling today

LOW VIBE ⊂⟨_____⟩⊃ **HIGH VIBE**

No matter how big or small . . .

What powerful word elevates my energy and why?

_____

_____

_____

MY MANIFESTO

_____

_____

_____

_____

Today I have done the below to support my journey . . .

VISUALIZE ●   SELF-CARE ●   POSITIVE TALK ●

Today I need to let go of . . .

_____

_____

. . . to help me manifest.

I AM CELEBRATED

What is my vibe like today?

Colour in how high vibe you are feeling today

**LOW
VIBE** ⟨_____⟩ **HIGH
VIBE**

No matter how big or small . . .

How can I show love and gratitude to myself today?

_____

_____

_____

MY MANIFESTO

_____

_____

_____

_____

Today I have done the below to support my journey . . .

VISUALIZE ⬤   SELF-CARE ⬤   POSITIVE TALK ⬤

Today I need to let go of . . .

_____

_____

. . . to help me manifest.

RAISE YOUR VIBE BINGO

Can you complete a row, column or diagonal using this unique bingo card? Uplift your energy and use it to manifest your wishes!

ATTRACT YOUR DESIRES

MAKE A WISH	VISUALIZE	MEDITATE	LISTEN TO MUSIC	SHOW GRATITUDE
THINK POSITIVE	SMILE	TAKE ACTION	BREATH-WORK	VISION BOARD
RE-FRAME THOUGHTS	AFFIRM	ASK THE UNIVERSE	LAUGH	JOURNAL
FOLLOW YOUR INTUITION	SPEND TIME IN NATURE	LIVE IN THE PRESENT	CONTROL YOUR EMOTIONS	HUG SOMEONE
TAKE TIME TO REST	SET AN INTENTION	MOVE YOUR BODY	DO A DIGITAL DETOX	DE-CLUTTER YOUR SPACE

I AM STABLE

What is my vibe like today?

Colour in how high vibe you are feeling today

**LOW
VIBE** ⟨⟩ **HIGH
VIBE**

No matter how big or small . . .

An activity that nourishes me is . . .

_____

_____

_____

MY MANIFESTO

_____

_____

_____

_____

Today I have done the below to support my journey . . .

VISUALIZE ⬤   SELF-CARE ⬤   POSITIVE TALK ⬤

Today I need to let go of . . .

_____

_____

. . . to help me manifest.

I AM A MAVERICK

What is my vibe like today?

Colour in how high vibe you are feeling today

LOW VIBE ⟨_____⟩ **HIGH VIBE**

No matter how big or small . . .

What did I recently overcome and how does it make me feel?

_____

_____

_____

MY MANIFESTO

_____

_____

_____

_____

Today I have done the below to support my journey . . .

VISUALIZE ●   SELF-CARE ●   POSITIVE TALK ●

Today I need to let go of . . .

_____

_____

. . . to help me manifest.

I AM PURE

What is my vibe like today?

Colour in how high vibe you are feeling today

**LOW
VIBE** (_____) **HIGH
VIBE**

No matter how big or small . . .

What is something I do to stay healthy and how does it make me feel?

_____

_____

_____

MY MANIFESTO

_____

_____

_____

_____

Today I have done the below to support my journey . . .

VISUALIZE ⬤   SELF-CARE ⬤   POSITIVE TALK ⬤

Today I need to let go of . . .

_____

_____

. . . to help me manifest.

MIND DUMP

 Take some time to clear your mind by writing down any thoughts that come to you – positive or negative. This act of release will help prevent these thoughts from hindering your progress as you move forward.

I AM A TRAILBLAZER

What is my vibe like today?

Colour in how high vibe you are feeling today

LOW VIBE ⟨_____⟩ **HIGH VIBE**

No matter how big or small . . .

What brings back a happy memory?

_____

_____

_____

MY MANIFESTO

_____

_____

_____

_____

Today I have done the below to support my journey . . .

VISUALIZE ●   SELF-CARE ●   POSITIVE TALK ●

Today I need to let go of . . .

_____

_____

. . . to help me manifest.

I AM STILL

What is my vibe like today?

Colour in how high vibe you are feeling today

LOW VIBE ⟨_____⟩ **HIGH VIBE**

No matter how big or small . . .

What makes me feel strong and why?

_____

_____

_____

MY MANIFESTO

_____

_____

_____

_____

Today I have done the below to support my journey . . .

VISUALIZE ●   SELF-CARE ●   POSITIVE TALK ●

Today I need to let go of . . .

_____

_____

. . . to help me manifest.

I AM ENOUGH

What is my vibe like today?

Colour in how high vibe you are feeling today

LOW
VIBE

HIGH
VIBE

No matter how big or small . . .

What is one thing that brings me ease?

_____

_____

_____

MY MANIFESTO

_____

_____

_____

_____

Today I have done the below to support my journey . . .

VISUALIZE ⬤   SELF-CARE ⬤   POSITIVE TALK ⬤

Today I need to let go of . . .

_____

_____

. . . to help me manifest.

I . . .

Finish the sentence to help you stay aligned with your manifestations, providing as much or as little detail as necessary to keep you focused on your desired outcome.

I AM

I CAN

I WILL

I HAVE

I BELIEVE

I RECEIVE

I AM COMPLETE

What is my vibe like today?

Colour in how high vibe you are feeling today

LOW VIBE ⟨_____⟩ **HIGH VIBE**

No matter how big or small . . .

Who is someone dear to me and why?

_____

_____

_____

MY MANIFESTO

_____

_____

_____

_____

Today I have done the below to support my journey . . .

VISUALIZE ⬤   SELF-CARE ⬤   POSITIVE TALK ⬤

Today I need to let go of . . .

_____

_____

. . . to help me manifest.

I AM IMPORTANT

What is my vibe like today?

Colour in how high vibe you are feeling today

LOW VIBE ⬭ **HIGH VIBE**

No matter how big or small . . .

What is a powerful book I recently read or listened to?

_____

_____

_____

MY MANIFESTO

_____

_____

_____

_____

Today I have done the below to support my journey . . .

VISUALIZE ⬤   SELF-CARE ⬤   POSITIVE TALK ⬤

Today I need to let go of . . .

_____

_____

. . . to help me manifest.

I AM AN EXPLORER

What is my vibe like today?

Colour in how high vibe you are feeling today

**LOW
VIBE** ⊂──────────────────────────────⊃ **HIGH
VIBE**

No matter how big or small . . .

What am I most looking forward to this week?

_____

_____

_____

MY MANIFESTO

_____

_____

_____

Today I have done the below to support my journey . . .

VISUALIZE ⬤   SELF-CARE ⬤   POSITIVE TALK ⬤

Today I need to let go of . . .

_____

_____

. . . to help me manifest.

A SPACE TO SCRIPT

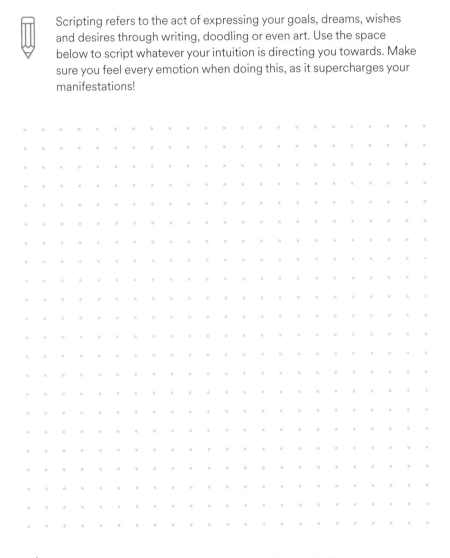 Scripting refers to the act of expressing your goals, dreams, wishes and desires through writing, doodling or even art. Use the space below to script whatever your intuition is directing you towards. Make sure you feel every emotion when doing this, as it supercharges your manifestations!

 Tip: Spend a few moments at the end to visualize and lock into place what you have scripted.

I AM ALIVE

What is my vibe like today?

Colour in how high vibe you are feeling today

**LOW
VIBE** ⊂_____⊃ **HIGH
VIBE**

No matter how big or small . . .

What is my favourite emotion to feel and why?

_____

_____

_____

MY MANIFESTO

_____

_____

_____

Today I have done the below to support my journey . . .

VISUALIZE ●   SELF-CARE ●   POSITIVE TALK ●

Today I need to let go of . . .

_____

_____

. . . to help me manifest.

I AM A GROUNDBREAKER

What is my vibe like today?

Colour in how high vibe you are feeling today

LOW VIBE ⟨────────────────────⟩ **HIGH VIBE**

No matter how big or small . . .

What is my favourite place in my home and why?

_____

_____

_____

MY MANIFESTO

_____

_____

_____

_____

Today I have done the below to support my journey . . .

VISUALIZE ⬤   SELF-CARE ⬤   POSITIVE TALK ⬤

Today I need to let go of . . .

_____

_____

. . . to help me manifest.

I AM DELIGHTED

What is my vibe like today?

Colour in how high vibe you are feeling today

LOW VIBE ⟨_____⟩ **HIGH VIBE**

No matter how big or small . . .

What is the most recent miracle that I experienced?

_____

_____

_____

MY MANIFESTO

_____

_____

_____

_____

Today I have done the below to support my journey . . .

VISUALIZE ●   SELF-CARE ●   POSITIVE TALK ●

Today I need to let go of . . .

_____

_____

. . . to help me manifest.

MY LIMITING BELIEFS

Overcome any limiting beliefs that may be hindering your ability to perceive all the opportunities available to you by practising this exercise to promote joy and appreciation.

A BELIEF I HAVE

WHERE DID IT COME FROM?

WHAT CAN I REPLACE IT WITH?

I AM A CHANGE-MAKER

What is my vibe like today?

Colour in how high vibe you are feeling today

**LOW
VIBE** ◖_____◗ **HIGH
VIBE**

No matter how big or small . . .

What is something that brings me happiness in the morning and why?

_____

_____

_____

MY MANIFESTO

_____

_____

_____

_____

Today I have done the below to support my journey . . .

VISUALIZE ●   SELF-CARE ●   POSITIVE TALK ●

Today I need to let go of . . .

_____

_____

_____

. . . to help me manifest.

I AM PROSPEROUS

What is my vibe like today?

Colour in how high vibe you are feeling today

LOW VIBE ⟨_____⟩ **HIGH VIBE**

No matter how big or small . . .

What is something that keeps me uplifted when I need it the most?

_____

_____

_____

MY MANIFESTO

_____

_____

_____

_____

Today I have done the below to support my journey . . .

VISUALIZE ⬤   SELF-CARE ⬤   POSITIVE TALK ⬤

Today I need to let go of . . .

_____

_____

. . . to help me manifest.

I AM REVOLUTIONARY

What is my vibe like today?

Colour in how high vibe you are feeling today

LOW VIBE ⟨_____⟩ **HIGH VIBE**

No matter how big or small . . .

Who is someone that shows me willpower?

_____

_____

_____

MY MANIFESTO

_____

_____

_____

_____

Today I have done the below to support my journey . . .

VISUALIZE ●   SELF-CARE ●   POSITIVE TALK ●

Today I need to let go of . . .

_____

_____

. . . to help me manifest.

FAKE IT TILL YOU MAKE IT

 How would you think if you manifested the things you wished for?
How would you look, sound and act? Use the space below to build
your future self. Use words, phrases, symbols or drawings to depict the
future you.

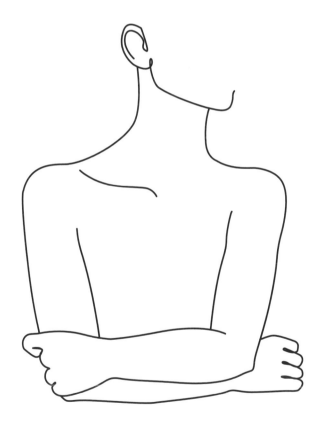

 Tip: *Make sure you FEEL and VISUALIZE everything you write down.*

I AM A DREAMER

What is my vibe like today?

Colour in how high vibe you are feeling today

**LOW
VIBE** ⟨_____⟩ **HIGH
VIBE**

No matter how big or small . . .

Who is someone that lets me be my authentic self?

_____

_____

_____

MY MANIFESTO

_____

_____

_____

_____

Today I have done the below to support my journey . . .

VISUALIZE ⬤   SELF-CARE ⬤   POSITIVE TALK ⬤

Today I need to let go of . . .

_____

_____

. . . to help me manifest.

I AM A GAME-CHANGER

What is my vibe like today?

Colour in how high vibe you are feeling today

LOW VIBE ⬭ **HIGH VIBE**

No matter how big or small . . .

What is one way I have grown for the better?

_____

_____

_____

MY MANIFESTO

_____

_____

_____

_____

Today I have done the below to support my journey . . .

VISUALIZE ⬤   SELF-CARE ⬤   POSITIVE TALK ⬤

Today I need to let go of . . .

_____

_____

. . . to help me manifest.

I AM LUMINOUS

What is my vibe like today?

Colour in how high vibe you are feeling today

LOW VIBE ⊂_____⊃ **HIGH VIBE**

No matter how big or small . . .

What do I love about the present moment and why?

_____

_____

_____

MY MANIFESTO

_____

_____

_____

Today I have done the below to support my journey . . .

VISUALIZE ⬤   SELF-CARE ⬤   POSITIVE TALK ⬤

Today I need to let go of . . .

_____

_____

. . . to help me manifest.

MANIFEST CHALLENGE

 Challenge yourself and raise your vibration today. Tick any of the below that you have managed to do recently. One is left blank for you to fill in with something that is personal to you.

CHOOSE A POSITIVE
AFFIRMATION TO
RECITE TODAY

LIVE TODAY AS IF
YOUR DREAM HAS
COME TRUE

TAKE ANOTHER
STEP TOWARDS
YOUR GOAL

WRITE FOUR THINGS
THAT YOU LOVE
ABOUT YOURSELF

DECLUTTER YOUR SPACE

SHOW GRATITUDE
TOWARDS SOMEONE

I AM AN ALCHEMIST

What is my vibe like today?

Colour in how high vibe you are feeling today

LOW VIBE ⟨ ⟩ **HIGH VIBE**

No matter how big or small . . .

How do I give myself permission to rest and recharge?

_____

_____

_____

MY MANIFESTO

_____

_____

_____

Today I have done the below to support my journey . . .

VISUALIZE ⬤   SELF-CARE ⬤   POSITIVE TALK ⬤

Today I need to let go of . . .

_____

_____

. . . to help me manifest.

I AM ATTRACTIVE

What is my vibe like today?

Colour in how high vibe you are feeling today

**LOW
VIBE** ⟮_____⟯ **HIGH
VIBE**

No matter how big or small . . .

What is something that went well for me today?

_____

_____

_____

MY MANIFESTO

_____

_____

_____

Today I have done the below to support my journey . . .

VISUALIZE ⬤   SELF-CARE ⬤   POSITIVE TALK ⬤

Today I need to let go of . . .

_____

_____

. . . to help me manifest.

I AM APPROACHABLE

What is my vibe like today?

Colour in how high vibe you are feeling today

LOW VIBE ◁⎯⎯⎯⎯⎯⎯⎯⎯⎯⎯⎯⎯⎯⎯⎯▷ **HIGH VIBE**

No matter how big or small . . .

What is a moment that I will always savour and why?

_____

_____

_____

MY MANIFESTO

_____

_____

_____

Today I have done the below to support my journey . . .

VISUALIZE ●　　　SELF-CARE ●　　　POSITIVE TALK ●

Today I need to let go of . . .

_____

_____

. . . to help me manifest.

30-DAY MANIFEST CHECK-IN

Check in with how your manifestation journey is going and notice anything that needs to be tweaked to keep you on track.

WHAT WENT WELL OVER THE LAST 30 DAYS?

HOW AM I FEELING ABOUT MY MANIFESTING JOURNEY SO FAR?

IS THERE ANYTHING I STRUGGLED WITH?

IS THERE ANYTHING I COULD DO TO SUPPORT MY MANIFESTATIONS?

I AM HEALING

What is my vibe like today?

Colour in how high vibe you are feeling today

LOW VIBE ⟨ _____ ⟩ **HIGH VIBE**

No matter how big or small . . .

What is one quality that makes me stand out?

_____

_____

_____

MY MANIFESTO

_____

_____

_____

_____

Today I have done the below to support my journey . . .

VISUALIZE ⬤   SELF-CARE ⬤   POSITIVE TALK ⬤

Today I need to let go of . . .

_____

_____

. . . to help me manifest.

I AM MAGIC

What is my vibe like today?

Colour in how high vibe you are feeling today

**LOW
VIBE** ⟨_____⟩ **HIGH
VIBE**

No matter how big or small . . .

What is something special I bring to this world?

_____

_____

_____

MY MANIFESTO

_____

_____

_____

_____

Today I have done the below to support my journey . . .

VISUALIZE ⚫   SELF-CARE ⚫   POSITIVE TALK ⚫

Today I need to let go of . . .

_____

_____

. . . to help me manifest.

I AM A MIRACLE-MAKER

What is my vibe like today?

Colour in how high vibe you are feeling today

**LOW
VIBE** ⟨⎯⎯⎯⎯⎯⎯⎯⎯⎯⎯⎯⎯⎯⎯⎯⎯⎯⎯⎯⎯⎯⎯⟩ **HIGH
VIBE**

No matter how big or small . . .

What am I grateful for about the environment I live in?

_____

_____

_____

MY MANIFESTO

_____

_____

_____

Today I have done the below to support my journey . . .

VISUALIZE ●   **SELF-CARE** ●   **POSITIVE TALK** ●

Today I need to let go of . . .

_____

_____

. . . to help me manifest.

CLAIM IT

Positive affirmations are a powerful tool that can really help in your manifesting journey. Write out an affirmation for something you would like to attract in your life and repeat it below on each line.

_____

_____

_____

_____

_____

_____

_____

_____

_____

_____

_____

_____

_____

_____

_____

_____

_____

Tip: *Recite your affirmation out loud. What you verbalize, you materialize.*

I AM MANIFESTING

What is my vibe like today?

Colour in how high vibe you are feeling today

**LOW
VIBE** ⬭ **HIGH
VIBE**

No matter how big or small . . .

What pastime brings me joy and how does it enrich my life?

_____

_____

_____

MY MANIFESTO

_____

_____

_____

_____

Today I have done the below to support my journey . . .

VISUALIZE ● SELF-CARE ● POSITIVE TALK ●

Today I need to let go of . . .

_____

_____

. . . to help me manifest.

I AM CHEERFUL

What is my vibe like today?

Colour in how high vibe you are feeling today

LOW VIBE ⟨_____⟩ **HIGH VIBE**

No matter how big or small . . .

Who is someone that has made a difference in my life and how?

_____

_____

_____

MY MANIFESTO

_____

_____

_____

_____

Today I have done the below to support my journey . . .

VISUALIZE ●   SELF-CARE ●   POSITIVE TALK ●

Today I need to let go of . . .

_____

_____

. . . to help me manifest.

I AM AWAKENED

What is my vibe like today?

Colour in how high vibe you are feeling today

LOW VIBE ⟨_____⟩ **HIGH VIBE**

No matter how big or small . . .

What skill has helped me in my life and how?

_____

_____

_____

MY MANIFESTO

_____

_____

_____

_____

Today I have done the below to support my journey . . .

VISUALIZE ⬤   SELF-CARE ⬤   POSITIVE TALK ⬤

Today I need to let go of . . .

_____

_____

. . . to help me manifest.

11 WISHES

 In numerology, the number 11 is considered powerful because it represents new beginnings, manifestations, and spiritual awakenings. Create a list of all your wishes and have faith in your aspirations. (It is OK to repeat your wishes, too!)

1. _____

2. _____

3. _____

4. _____

5. _____

6. _____

7. _____

8. _____

9. _____

10. _____

11. _____

 Tip: You can use one-word wishes for this activity.

I AM MIRACULOUS

What is my vibe like today?

Colour in how high vibe you are feeling today

LOW VIBE ⟨_____⟩ **HIGH VIBE**

No matter how big or small . . .

A favourite memory I have of a special occasion is . . .

_____

_____

_____

MY MANIFESTO

_____

_____

_____

_____

Today I have done the below to support my journey . . .

VISUALIZE ●   SELF-CARE ●   POSITIVE TALK ●

Today I need to let go of . . .

_____

_____

. . . to help me manifest.

I AM DIVINE

What is my vibe like today?

Colour in how high vibe you are feeling today

**LOW
VIBE** ⟨_____⟩ **HIGH
VIBE**

No matter how big or small . . .

Something that helped me expand my understanding of the world is . . .

_____

_____

_____

MY MANIFESTO

_____

_____

_____

_____

Today I have done the below to support my journey . . .

VISUALIZE ●   SELF-CARE ●   POSITIVE TALK ●

Today I need to let go of . . .

_____

_____

. . . to help me manifest.

I AM THRIVING

What is my vibe like today?

Colour in how high vibe you are feeling today

**LOW
VIBE** ⬭ **HIGH
VIBE**

No matter how big or small . . .

The last good deed I did was . . .

_____

_____

_____

MY MANIFESTO

_____

_____

_____

_____

Today I have done the below to support my journey . . .

VISUALIZE ⬤   SELF-CARE ⬤   POSITIVE TALK ⬤

Today I need to let go of . . .

_____

_____

. . . to help me manifest.

MANIFEST WORDSEARCH

Take some time away from your digital device and search for some empowering manifesting words to keep your mind topped up with positivity!

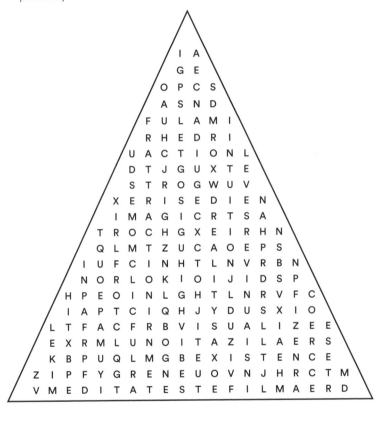

VIBRATION	ATTRACTION	DESIRE	CREATE	VISUALIZE
ACTION	FULFIL	MAGIC	UNIVERSE	ENERGY
LET GO	HIGH VIBE	WISH	REALITY	DREAM LIFE
REALIZATION	INTUITION	GUIDANCE	MEDITATE	EXISTENCE

 Tip: Go to *The Rising Circle* YouTube channel for more guided meditations.

I AM ENGAGING

What is my vibe like today?

Colour in how high vibe you are feeling today

LOW VIBE ⟨_____⟩ **HIGH VIBE**

No matter how big or small . . .

I love my body because . . .

_____

_____

_____

MY MANIFESTO

_____

_____

_____

_____

Today I have done the below to support my journey . . .

VISUALIZE ⬤   SELF-CARE ⬤   POSITIVE TALK ⬤

Today I need to let go of . . .

_____

_____

. . . to help me manifest.

I AM SUPPORTIVE

What is my vibe like today?

Colour in how high vibe you are feeling today

LOW VIBE ⟨_____⟩ **HIGH VIBE**

No matter how big or small . . .

What memory do I appreciate and how has it shaped who I am today?

_____

_____

_____

MY MANIFESTO

_____

_____

_____

_____

Today I have done the below to support my journey . . .

VISUALIZE ⚪   SELF-CARE ⚪   POSITIVE TALK ⚪

Today I need to let go of . . .

_____

_____

. . . to help me manifest.

I AM SENSATIONAL

What is my vibe like today?

Colour in how high vibe you are feeling today

LOW
VIBE
HIGH
VIBE

No matter how big or small . . .

What is something that gives me a sense of purpose and why?

_____

_____

_____

MY MANIFESTO

_____

_____

_____

_____

Today I have done the below to support my journey . . .

VISUALIZE ●   SELF-CARE ●   POSITIVE TALK ●

Today I need to let go of . . .

_____

_____

. . . to help me manifest.

VIBING HIGH

To manifest our desires, we need to raise our vibration to a level that resonates with them. Identify one thing that brings positive energy into your life and helps you stay aligned with your goals. Write it down and make it a regular part of your routine to maintain a high frequency.

ONE MEMORY THAT MAKES ME LAUGH

ONE THING I BELIEVE IN

ONE SONG THAT I LOVE LISTENING TO

ONE PERSON THAT I LOVE BEING AROUND

ONE MEAL THAT MAKES ME HAPPY

ONE ACTIVITY I AM ALWAYS UP FOR

ONE MOVIE I LOVE WATCHING

I AM PHENOMENAL

What is my vibe like today?

Colour in how high vibe you are feeling today

**LOW
VIBE** ⟨⟩ **HIGH
VIBE**

No matter how big or small . . .

What sort of gratification do I get when I have achieved something?

_____

_____

_____

MY MANIFESTO

_____

_____

_____

_____

Today I have done the below to support my journey . . .

VISUALIZE ⬤   SELF-CARE ⬤   POSITIVE TALK ⬤

Today I need to let go of . . .

_____

_____

. . . to help me manifest.

I AM EXTRAORDINARY

What is my vibe like today?

Colour in how high vibe you are feeling today

LOW VIBE ⬭ **HIGH VIBE**

No matter how big or small . . .

Who is someone that gives me guidance when I need it?

_____

_____

_____

MY MANIFESTO

_____

_____

_____

_____

Today I have done the below to support my journey . . .

VISUALIZE ⬤   SELF-CARE ⬤   POSITIVE TALK ⬤

Today I need to let go of . . .

_____

_____

. . . to help me manifest.

I AM REMARKABLE

What is my vibe like today?

Colour in how high vibe you are feeling today

LOW
VIBE ⟨_____⟩ HIGH
VIBE

No matter how big or small . . .

What is something I am passionate about and why?

_____

_____

_____

MY MANIFESTO

_____

_____

_____

_____

Today I have done the below to support my journey . . .

VISUALIZE ●   SELF-CARE ●   POSITIVE TALK ●

Today I need to let go of . . .

_____

_____

. . . to help me manifest.

TUNING INTO UNIVERSAL FM

 Meditation helps to quiet the mind, reduce stress, increase focus and connect you with the Universe. Check out our meditation channel to tune in with the Universe and align with the energy of your desires to manifest them effortlessly.

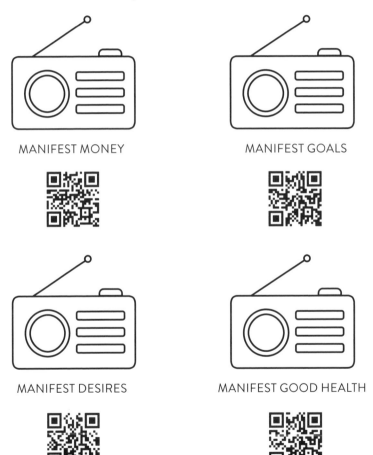

MANIFEST MONEY

MANIFEST GOALS

MANIFEST DESIRES

MANIFEST GOOD HEALTH

 Tip: *Go to The Rising Circle YouTube channel for more guided meditations.*

I AM MAGNIFICENT

What is my vibe like today?

Colour in how high vibe you are feeling today

LOW VIBE ⸨ ⸩ **HIGH VIBE**

No matter how big or small . . .

What is a thoughtful thing someone has done for me recently?

_____

_____

_____

MY MANIFESTO

_____

_____

_____

_____

Today I have done the below to support my journey . . .

VISUALIZE ⬤   SELF-CARE ⬤   POSITIVE TALK ⬤

Today I need to let go of . . .

_____

_____

. . . to help me manifest.

I AM SPECTACULAR

What is my vibe like today?

Colour in how high vibe you are feeling today

LOW VIBE ⊂ ⊃ **HIGH VIBE**

No matter how big or small . . .

A favourite memory I have of a loved one is . . .

_____

_____

_____

MY MANIFESTO

_____

_____

_____

_____

Today I have done the below to support my journey . . .

VISUALIZE ●   SELF-CARE ●   POSITIVE TALK ●

Today I need to let go of . . .

_____

_____

. . . to help me manifest.

I AM MAJESTIC

What is my vibe like today?

Colour in how high vibe you are feeling today

LOW VIBE ⟨_____⟩ **HIGH VIBE**

No matter how big or small . . .

Something I am excited to try is . . .

_____

_____

_____

MY MANIFESTO

_____

_____

_____

_____

Today I have done the below to support my journey . . .

VISUALIZE ⬤   SELF-CARE ⬤   POSITIVE TALK ⬤

Today I need to let go of . . .

_____

_____

. . . to help me manifest.

A SPACE TO SCRIPT

Scripting refers to the act of expressing your goals, dreams, wishes and desires through writing, doodling or even art. Use the space below to script whatever your intuition is directing you towards. Make sure you feel every emotion when doing this, as it supercharges your manifestations!

Tip: Spend a few moments at the end to visualize and lock into place what you have scripted.

I AM HUMOROUS

What is my vibe like today?

Colour in how high vibe you are feeling today

**LOW
VIBE** ⊂⎯⎯⎯⎯⎯⎯⎯⎯⎯⎯⎯⎯⎯⎯⎯⎯⎯⎯⎯⎯⎯⎯⎯⎯⎯⎯⊃ **HIGH
VIBE**

No matter how big or small . . .

What place would I like to visit and why?

_____

_____

_____

MY MANIFESTO

_____

_____

_____

_____

Today I have done the below to support my journey . . .

VISUALIZE ⬤   SELF-CARE ⬤   POSITIVE TALK ⬤

Today I need to let go of . . .

_____

_____

. . . to help me manifest.

I AM EXCEPTIONAL

What is my vibe like today?

Colour in how high vibe you are feeling today

**LOW
VIBE** (_____) **HIGH
VIBE**

No matter how big or small . . .

A time when I felt a deep sense of connection with someone was . . .

_____

_____

_____

MY MANIFESTO

_____

_____

_____

_____

Today I have done the below to support my journey . . .

VISUALIZE ●   SELF-CARE ●   POSITIVE TALK ●

Today I need to let go of . . .

_____

_____

. . . to help me manifest.

I AM INCREDIBLE

What is my vibe like today?

Colour in how high vibe you are feeling today

LOW VIBE ⬭⬭⬭⬭⬭⬭⬭⬭⬭⬭⬭⬭⬭ **HIGH VIBE**

No matter how big or small...

What is a small act of kindness I can do for myself today?

_____

_____

_____

MY MANIFESTO

_____

_____

_____

_____

Today I have done the below to support my journey...

VISUALIZE ⬤   SELF-CARE ⬤   POSITIVE TALK ⬤

Today I need to let go of...

_____

_____

... to help me manifest.

WOULDN'T IT BE NICE

 This technique by Esther and Jerry Hicks involves visualizing the things you desire by framing them in a question that starts with 'Wouldn't it be nice if . . . ' It will help you focus on the feeling of having your desired outcome and put you in an optimistic state of mind. Finish off the sentences and claim your thoughts as if they were already true.

WOULDN'T IT BE NICE IF . . . _____

_____

WOULDN'T IT BE NICE IF . . . _____

_____

WOULDN'T IT BE NICE IF . . . _____

_____

WOULDN'T IT BE NICE IF . . . _____

_____

WOULDN'T IT BE NICE IF . . . _____

_____

WOULDN'T IT BE NICE IF . . . _____

_____

WOULDN'T IT BE NICE IF . . . _____

_____

WOULDN'T IT BE NICE IF . . . _____

_____

I AM FANTASTIC

What is my vibe like today?

Colour in how high vibe you are feeling today

LOW VIBE ⟨_____⟩ **HIGH VIBE**

No matter how big or small . . .

What physical activity or exercise do I enjoy and why?

_____

_____

_____

MY MANIFESTO

_____

_____

_____

Today I have done the below to support my journey . . .

VISUALIZE ●   SELF-CARE ●   POSITIVE TALK ●

Today I need to let go of . . .

_____

_____

. . . to help me manifest.

I AM WONDERFUL

What is my vibe like today?

Colour in how high vibe you are feeling today

LOW VIBE ⟨_____⟩ **HIGH VIBE**

No matter how big or small . . .

A meaningful gift I have received is . . .

_____

_____

_____

MY MANIFESTO

_____

_____

_____

_____

Today I have done the below to support my journey . . .

VISUALIZE ⬤   SELF-CARE ⬤   POSITIVE TALK ⬤

Today I need to let go of . . .

_____

_____

. . . to help me manifest.

I AM AMAZING

What is my vibe like today?

Colour in how high vibe you are feeling today

LOW VIBE ⊂================================⊃ **HIGH VIBE**

No matter how big or small . . .

A happy surprise I recently experienced is . . .

_____

_____

_____

MY MANIFESTO

_____

_____

_____

_____

Today I have done the below to support my journey . . .

VISUALIZE ●   SELF-CARE ●   POSITIVE TALK ●

Today I need to let go of . . .

_____

_____

. . . to help me manifest.

WORD SCRAMBLE

 Unscramble to unveil the powerful words below.

WLA FO BIIRATNVO ➡️

OLFWLO ITOITIUNN ➡️

HGIH REYGEN ➡️

FMSEITAN MADSER ➡️

READ NERIUVES ➡️

I AM ASTONISHING

What is my vibe like today?

Colour in how high vibe you are feeling today

LOW VIBE ⊂⎯⎯⎯⎯⎯⎯⎯⎯⎯⎯⎯⎯⎯⎯⎯⎯⊃ **HIGH VIBE**

No matter how big or small . . .

What is something I find beautiful and why?

_____

_____

_____

MY MANIFESTO

_____

_____

_____

_____

Today I have done the below to support my journey . . .

VISUALIZE ⚫   **SELF-CARE** ⚫   **POSITIVE TALK** ⚫

Today I need to let go of . . .

_____

_____

. . . to help me manifest.

I AM MARVELLOUS

What is my vibe like today?

Colour in how high vibe you are feeling today

LOW VIBE ⊂━━━━━━━━━━━━━━━━━━━━━━━⊃ **HIGH VIBE**

No matter how big or small . . .

A time when I made a positive difference in someone else's life was . . .

_____

_____

_____

MY MANIFESTO

_____

_____

_____

_____

Today I have done the below to support my journey . . .

VISUALIZE ●   SELF-CARE ●   POSITIVE TALK ●

Today I need to let go of . . .

_____

_____

. . . to help me manifest.

I AM RESPECTED

What is my vibe like today?

Colour in how high vibe you are feeling today

LOW VIBE ⟨ ⟩ **HIGH VIBE**

No matter how big or small . . .

A favourite memory from a past trip is . . .

_____

_____

_____

MY MANIFESTO

_____

_____

_____

_____

Today I have done the below to support my journey . . .

VISUALIZE ●   SELF-CARE ●   POSITIVE TALK ●

Today I need to let go of . . .

_____

_____

. . . to help me manifest.

AFFIRMATION COLOURING

Colouring can be relaxing and satisfying. Let your creativity flow by colouring in this powerful affirmation and allow it to manifest.

I AM PURPOSEFUL

What is my vibe like today?

Colour in how high vibe you are feeling today

LOW
VIBE
HIGH
VIBE

No matter how big or small . . .

What is the kindest thing I have done for myself?

_____

_____

_____

MY MANIFESTO

_____

_____

_____

Today I have done the below to support my journey . . .

VISUALIZE ⬤   SELF-CARE ⬤   POSITIVE TALK ⬤

Today I need to let go of . . .

_____

_____

. . . to help me manifest.

I AM INQUISITIVE

What is my vibe like today?

Colour in how high vibe you are feeling today

LOW VIBE ⊂⊃ **HIGH VIBE**

No matter how big or small . . .

What is something helpful I can say to myself right now?

_____

_____

_____

MY MANIFESTO

_____

_____

_____

_____

Today I have done the below to support my journey . . .

VISUALIZE ●   SELF-CARE ●   POSITIVE TALK ●

Today I need to let go of . . .

_____

_____

. . . to help me manifest.

I AM MIND-BLOWING

What is my vibe like today?

Colour in how high vibe you are feeling today

**LOW
VIBE** ⟨_____⟩ **HIGH
VIBE**

No matter how big or small...

A time when I received a compliment that made me feel good was...

_____

_____

_____

MY MANIFESTO

_____

_____

_____

_____

Today I have done the below to support my journey...

VISUALIZE ●   SELF-CARE ●   POSITIVE TALK ●

Today I need to let go of...

_____

_____

... to help me manifest.

30-DAY MANIFEST CHECK-IN

Check in with how your manifestation journey is going and notice anything that needs to be tweaked to keep you on track.

WHAT WENT WELL OVER THE LAST 30 DAYS?

HOW AM I FEELING ABOUT MY MANIFESTING JOURNEY SO FAR?

IS THERE ANYTHING I STRUGGLED WITH?

IS THERE ANYTHING I COULD DO TO SUPPORT MY MANIFESTATIONS?

I AM DESERVING

What is my vibe like today?

Colour in how high vibe you are feeling today

LOW VIBE ⟨　　　　　　　　　　　　　　　　　⟩ **HIGH VIBE**

No matter how big or small . . .

A moment when I felt proud of my own strength was . . .

_____

_____

_____

MY MANIFESTO

_____

_____

_____

_____

Today I have done the below to support my journey . . .

VISUALIZE ●　　　SELF-CARE ●　　　POSITIVE TALK ●

Today I need to let go of . . .

_____

_____

. . . to help me manifest.

I AM ENLIGHTENED

What is my vibe like today?

Colour in how high vibe you are feeling today

LOW VIBE ◖_____◗ **HIGH VIBE**

No matter how big or small . . .

What is a favourite memory I have of spending time outdoors and why?

_____

_____

_____

MY MANIFESTO

_____

_____

_____

_____

Today I have done the below to support my journey . . .

VISUALIZE ●   SELF-CARE ●   POSITIVE TALK ●

Today I need to let go of . . .

_____

_____

. . . to help me manifest.

I AM ETHEREAL

What is my vibe like today?

Colour in how high vibe you are feeling today

LOW VIBE ⟨──────────────────────────────⟩ **HIGH VIBE**

No matter how big or small . . .

A time when I felt inspired by someone else's creativity was . . .

_____

_____

_____

MY MANIFESTO

_____

_____

_____

Today I have done the below to support my journey . . .

VISUALIZE ⬤   SELF-CARE ⬤   POSITIVE TALK ⬤

Today I need to let go of . . .

_____

_____

. . . to help me manifest.

CLAIM IT

Positive affirmations are a powerful tool that can really help in your manifesting journey. Write out an affirmation for something you would like to attract in your life and repeat it below on each line.

_____

_____

_____

_____

_____

_____

_____

_____

_____

_____

_____

_____

_____

_____

_____

_____

_____

 Tip: _Recite your affirmation out loud. What you verbalize, you materialize._

I AM HEAVENLY

What is my vibe like today?

Colour in how high vibe you are feeling today

LOW VIBE ⟨ ⟩ **HIGH VIBE**

No matter how big or small . . .

A moment when I felt completely carefree was . . .

_____

_____

_____

MY MANIFESTO

_____

_____

_____

_____

Today I have done the below to support my journey . . .

VISUALIZE ⚫   SELF-CARE ⚫   POSITIVE TALK ⚫

Today I need to let go of . . .

_____

_____

. . . to help me manifest.

I AM APPRECIATED

What is my vibe like today?

Colour in how high vibe you are feeling today

LOW VIBE ⊂───────────────────────────────────⊃ **HIGH VIBE**

No matter how big or small . . .

A time I received unexpected recognition for something I did was . . .

_____

_____

_____

MY MANIFESTO

_____

_____

_____

_____

Today I have done the below to support my journey . . .

VISUALIZE ⬤   SELF-CARE ⬤   POSITIVE TALK ⬤

Today I need to let go of . . .

_____

_____

. . . to help me manifest.

I AM PEACEFUL

What is my vibe like today?

Colour in how high vibe you are feeling today

**LOW
VIBE** ⊂⎯⎯⎯⎯⎯⎯⎯⎯⎯⎯⎯⎯⎯⎯⎯⎯⎯⎯⎯⊃ **HIGH
VIBE**

No matter how big or small . . .

What is something that brings me happiness in the evening and why?

_____

_____

_____

MY MANIFESTO

_____

_____

_____

_____

Today I have done the below to support my journey . . .

VISUALIZE ⬤   SELF-CARE ⬤   POSITIVE TALK ⬤

Today I need to let go of . . .

_____

_____

. . . to help me manifest.

DRINK IT

This water manifestation technique involves charging water with your intentions and then consuming it. The idea behind this is that water has the ability to hold energetic vibrations and can be programmed with your intentions. By drinking the water in your daily life, you are infusing your body and surroundings with the energy of your intentions, thus helping to attract your desired outcome. Simply follow the instructions below.

1. Grab a glass of water, a piece of paper, a pen and some sticky tape.

2. Write your affirmation on the paper and stick it onto the glass.

3. Hold the glass with both hands and close your eyes.

4. Take a deep breath, focusing your attention on the water.

5. Speak your affirmation to the water.

6. Visualize the positive energy flowing into the water as you speak.

7. Sip your water and feel as if you already have your desire.

8. Continue to focus on positive thoughts and feelings throughout the day as you drink your water.

 Tip: *Make sure you refill your glass throughout the day.*

I AM HARMONIOUS

What is my vibe like today?

Colour in how high vibe you are feeling today

LOW VIBE ⊂⟍⟍⟍⟍⟍⟍⟍⟍⟍⟍⟍⟍⟍⟍⟍⟍⟍⟍⟍⟍⟍⟍⟍⟍⟍⟍⟍⟍⊃ **HIGH VIBE**

No matter how big or small . . .

What is something that really boosts my confidence?

_____

_____

_____

MY MANIFESTO

_____

_____

_____

_____

Today I have done the below to support my journey . . .

VISUALIZE ●   SELF-CARE ●   POSITIVE TALK ●

Today I need to let go of . . .

_____

_____

. . . to help me manifest.

I AM BLISSFUL

What is my vibe like today?

Colour in how high vibe you are feeling today

LOW VIBE ⬭⬭⬭⬭⬭⬭⬭⬭⬭⬭⬭⬭⬭⬭⬭⬭ **HIGH VIBE**

No matter how big or small . . .

A time when I was fully immersed in the moment was . . .

_____

_____

_____

MY MANIFESTO

_____

_____

_____

_____

Today I have done the below to support my journey . . .

VISUALIZE ⬤   SELF-CARE ⬤   POSITIVE TALK ⬤

Today I need to let go of . . .

_____

_____

. . . to help me manifest.

I AM FLOURISHING

What is my vibe like today?

Colour in how high vibe you are feeling today

LOW VIBE ⟨_____⟩ **HIGH VIBE**

No matter how big or small . . .

What is something that gives me the opportunity to connect?

_____

_____

_____

MY MANIFESTO

_____

_____

_____

_____

Today I have done the below to support my journey . . .

VISUALIZE ●   SELF-CARE ●   POSITIVE TALK ●

Today I need to let go of . . .

_____

_____

_____ . . . to help me manifest.

MANIFEST CHALLENGE

 Challenge yourself and raise your vibration today. Tick any of the below that you have managed to do recently. One is left blank for you to fill in with something that is personal to you.

MEDITATE TO
MANIFEST YOUR
DESIRE

FOCUS
ON ONE
AFFIRMATION

SPEND TIME WITH NATURE

LISTEN TO
YOUR FAVOURITE
SONG

CARRY OUT
AN ACT OF
SELF-CARE

READ SOMETHING
INSPIRING

I AM GLOWING

What is my vibe like today?

Colour in how high vibe you are feeling today

**LOW
VIBE** ⬭ **HIGH
VIBE**

No matter how big or small . . .

What is a moment of happiness I experienced recently?

_____

_____

_____

MY MANIFESTO

_____

_____

_____

_____

Today I have done the below to support my journey . . .

VISUALIZE ● SELF-CARE ● POSITIVE TALK ●

Today I need to let go of . . .

_____

_____

. . . to help me manifest.

I AM VIBRANT

What is my vibe like today?

Colour in how high vibe you are feeling today

**LOW
VIBE** ⟨ _____ ⟩ **HIGH
VIBE**

No matter how big or small . . .

Someone who has been there for me through thick and thin is . . .

_____

_____

_____

MY MANIFESTO

_____

_____

_____

_____

Today I have done the below to support my journey . . .

VISUALIZE ●   SELF-CARE ●   POSITIVE TALK ●

Today I need to let go of . . .

_____

_____

. . . to help me manifest.

I AM IN TUNE

What is my vibe like today?

Colour in how high vibe you are feeling today

LOW
VIBE ⸨ _____ ⸩ HIGH
VIBE

No matter how big or small . . .

What is one thing I have today that I dreamt of having in the past?

_____

_____

_____

MY MANIFESTO

_____

_____

_____

_____

Today I have done the below to support my journey . . .

VISUALIZE ● SELF-CARE ● POSITIVE TALK ●

Today I need to let go of . . .

_____

_____

. . . to help me manifest.

I ALREADY HAVE IT

To manifest something, you need to bring it to your reality (AKA the Law of Assumption) and to do this you need to act as if you already have it. So, make your dream a reality, starting now!

I HAVE . . .

IT MAKES ME FEEL . . .

I AM GOING TO CELEBRATE BY . . .

I AM EVERYTHING

What is my vibe like today?

Colour in how high vibe you are feeling today

LOW
VIBE ⊂⊃ HIGH
VIBE

No matter how big or small . . .

A value I hold that I am grateful for is . . .

_____

_____

_____

MY MANIFESTO

_____

_____

_____

_____

Today I have done the below to support my journey . . .

VISUALIZE ●   SELF-CARE ●   POSITIVE TALK ●

Today I need to let go of . . .

_____

_____

. . . to help me manifest.

I AM REBORN

What is my vibe like today?

Colour in how high vibe you are feeling today

LOW
VIBE ⟨_____⟩ HIGH
VIBE

No matter how big or small . . .

In what way have I been able to give back to others?

_____

_____

_____

MY MANIFESTO

_____

_____

_____

_____

Today I have done the below to support my journey . . .

VISUALIZE ⬤   SELF-CARE ⬤   POSITIVE TALK ⬤

Today I need to let go of . . .

_____

_____

. . . to help me manifest.

I AM UNIQUE

What is my vibe like today?

Colour in how high vibe you are feeling today

LOW VIBE ⟨_____⟩ **HIGH VIBE**

No matter how big or small . . .

A time when someone showed me grace was . . .

_____

_____

_____

MY MANIFESTO

_____

_____

_____

_____

Today I have done the below to support my journey . . .

VISUALIZE ⬤   SELF-CARE ⬤   POSITIVE TALK ⬤

Today I need to let go of . . .

_____

_____

. . . to help me manifest.

DEFINE SUCCESS

 Defining success is an essential step towards achieving it. Reflect on what success means to you, and write down your responses below to stay focused on your goals.

WHAT DOES SUCCESS MEAN TO ME?

WHAT DOES SUCCESS LOOK LIKE IN MY LIFE?

WHAT DOES SUCCESS LOOK LIKE IN MY HEALTH AND WELL-BEING?

WHAT DOES SUCCESS LOOK LIKE IN MY RELATIONSHIPS?

WHAT DOES SUCCESS LOOK LIKE IN MY GROWTH?

WHAT DOES SUCCESS LOOK LIKE IN MY CAREER?

I AM EXUBERANT

What is my vibe like today?

Colour in how high vibe you are feeling today

LOW VIBE ⟨ _____ ⟩ **HIGH VIBE**

No matter how big or small . . .

What habit brings me peace and why?

_____

_____

_____

MY MANIFESTO

_____

_____

_____

Today I have done the below to support my journey . . .

VISUALIZE ⬤   SELF-CARE ⬤   POSITIVE TALK ⬤

Today I need to let go of . . .

_____

_____

. . . to help me manifest.

I AM ENTHUSIASTIC

What is my vibe like today?

Colour in how high vibe you are feeling today

LOW VIBE (_____) **HIGH VIBE**

No matter how big or small . . .

What form of self-expression am I grateful for and why?

_____

_____

_____

MY MANIFESTO

_____

_____

_____

_____

Today I have done the below to support my journey . . .

VISUALIZE ●   SELF-CARE ●   POSITIVE TALK ●

Today I need to let go of . . .

_____

_____

. . . to help me manifest.

I AM BRILLIANT

What is my vibe like today?

Colour in how high vibe you are feeling today

**LOW
VIBE** ⟨_____⟩ **HIGH
VIBE**

No matter how big or small . . .

A moment when I practised patience was . . .

_____

_____

_____

MY MANIFESTO

_____

_____

_____

Today I have done the below to support my journey . . .

VISUALIZE ●   SELF-CARE ●   POSITIVE TALK ●

Today I need to let go of . . .

_____

_____

. . . to help me manifest.

A SPACE TO SCRIPT

Scripting refers to the act of expressing your goals, dreams, wishes and desires through writing, doodling or even art. Use the space below to script whatever your intuition is directing you towards. Make sure you feel every emotion when doing this, as it supercharges your manifestations!

 Tip: *Spend a few moments at the end to visualize and lock into place what you have scripted.*

_____

I AM GLORIOUS

What is my vibe like today?

Colour in how high vibe you are feeling today

LOW
VIBE ⟨ _____ ⟩ HIGH
VIBE

No matter how big or small . . .

Something that I am grateful for in my daily life is . . .

_____

_____

_____

MY MANIFESTO

_____

_____

_____

_____

Today I have done the below to support my journey . . .

VISUALIZE ⬤   SELF-CARE ⬤   POSITIVE TALK ⬤

Today I need to let go of . . .

_____

_____

. . . to help me manifest.

I AM INSPIRED

What is my vibe like today?

Colour in how high vibe you are feeling today

LOW VIBE ⬭ **HIGH VIBE**

No matter how big or small . . .

A time when I got to pursue my passion was . . .

_____

_____

_____

MY MANIFESTO

_____

_____

_____

_____

Today I have done the below to support my journey . . .

VISUALIZE ●   SELF-CARE ●   POSITIVE TALK ●

Today I need to let go of . . .

_____

_____

. . . to help me manifest.

I AM OVERFLOWING

What is my vibe like today?

Colour in how high vibe you are feeling today

LOW
VIBE ⟨_____⟩ HIGH
VIBE

No matter how big or small . . .

A recent experience where I felt connected to others is . . .

_____

_____

_____

MY MANIFESTO

_____

_____

_____

Today I have done the below to support my journey . . .

VISUALIZE ⚫   SELF-CARE ⚫   POSITIVE TALK ⚫

Today I need to let go of . . .

_____

_____

. . . to help me manifest.

GRATITUDE LIST

 We are blessed with so much in our lives that we often overlook. This is your chance to highlight these things and enter a genuine state of gratitude to attract yet more things to be grateful for. List whatever people, places, objects or even memories that come to mind.

-
-
-
-
-
-
-
-
-
-
-
-
-
-
-
-
-

I AM PROTECTED

What is my vibe like today?

Colour in how high vibe you are feeling today

LOW
VIBE ⟨_____⟩ HIGH
VIBE

No matter how big or small . . .

What is a place that makes me feel secure?

_____

_____

_____

MY MANIFESTO

_____

_____

_____

_____

Today I have done the below to support my journey . . .

VISUALIZE ⬤   SELF-CARE ⬤   POSITIVE TALK ⬤

Today I need to let go of . . .

_____

_____

. . . to help me manifest.

I AM HONOURABLE

What is my vibe like today?

Colour in how high vibe you are feeling today

LOW VIBE ⟨_____⟩ **HIGH VIBE**

No matter how big or small . . .

A quality that I most admire about others is . . .

_____

_____

_____

MY MANIFESTO

_____

_____

_____

_____

Today I have done the below to support my journey . . .

VISUALIZE ⚪   SELF-CARE ⚪   POSITIVE TALK ⚪

Today I need to let go of . . .

_____

_____

. . . to help me manifest.

I AM ALIGNED

What is my vibe like today?

Colour in how high vibe you are feeling today

LOW VIBE (_____) **HIGH VIBE**

No matter how big or small . . .

A treat that brings me joy is . . .

_____

_____

_____

MY MANIFESTO

_____

_____

_____

Today I have done the below to support my journey . . .

VISUALIZE ⬤   SELF-CARE ⬤   POSITIVE TALK ⬤

Today I need to let go of . . .

_____

_____

. . . to help me manifest.

BOOK OF POSITIVE ASPECTS

 The Book of Positive Aspects is a technique developed by Esther and Jerry Hicks. The process involves focusing on positive aspects of a person, situation or thing, to train the mind to look for the positive in everything. Write the subject (e.g. nature) in the left-hand column and populate the rest of the boxes to feel a shift in your vibration.

THE POSITIVE ASPECT OF	WHAT DO I LIKE ABOUT YOU?	WHY DO I LOVE YOU SO MUCH?	WHAT ARE YOUR POSITIVE ASPECTS?

THE POSITIVE ASPECT OF	WHAT DO I LIKE ABOUT YOU?	WHY DO I LOVE YOU SO MUCH?	WHAT ARE YOUR POSITIVE ASPECTS?

THE POSITIVE ASPECT OF	WHAT DO I LIKE ABOUT YOU?	WHY DO I LOVE YOU SO MUCH?	WHAT ARE YOUR POSITIVE ASPECTS?

I AM PRECIOUS

What is my vibe like today?

Colour in how high vibe you are feeling today

LOW
VIBE ⊂⟨_____⟩ HIGH
VIBE

No matter how big or small . . .

A moment when I received encouragement from someone was . . .

_____

_____

_____

MY MANIFESTO

_____

_____

_____

_____

Today I have done the below to support my journey . . .

VISUALIZE ●   SELF-CARE ●   POSITIVE TALK ●

Today I need to let go of . . .

_____

_____

. . . to help me manifest.

I AM GROWING

What is my vibe like today?

Colour in how high vibe you are feeling today

LOW VIBE ⬭_____⬭ **HIGH VIBE**

No matter how big or small . . .

An environment that has a special meaning to me is . . .

_____

_____

_____

MY MANIFESTO

_____

_____

_____

_____

Today I have done the below to support my journey . . .

VISUALIZE ⬤   SELF-CARE ⬤   POSITIVE TALK ⬤

Today I need to let go of . . .

_____

_____

. . . to help me manifest.

I AM SKILLFUL

What is my vibe like today?

Colour in how high vibe you are feeling today

**LOW
VIBE** ⟨_____⟩ **HIGH
VIBE**

No matter how big or small . . .

What is one positive word I can use to describe myself and why?

_____

_____

_____

MY MANIFESTO

_____

_____

_____

Today I have done the below to support my journey . . .

VISUALIZE ⬤   SELF-CARE ⬤   POSITIVE TALK ⬤

Today I need to let go of . . .

_____

_____

. . . to help me manifest.

BREATHWORK

Conscious breathing can help you access deeper states of consciousness to shorten the path to your desired outcomes. Experience the magic of breathwork by giving this short exercise a go.

1. Find a quiet and comfortable place where you can sit or lie down without being disturbed.

2. Take a few deep breaths and focus on releasing any tension or stress from your body.

3. Close your eyes and visualize what you want to manifest in your life. See it clearly in your mind's eye and feel the emotions of having it already.

4. Take a slow, deep breath in through your nose, filling your lungs with air. Hold your breath for a few seconds.

5. Visualize the manifestation becoming a reality as you hold your breath.

6. Slowly exhale through your mouth, releasing any doubts or negative thoughts you may have.

7. Repeat steps 4 to 6 until you feel a sense of calm and clarity.

 Tip: *If you enjoy this, add this to your High Vibe Hacks Kit on page 8.*

I AM AWARE

What is my vibe like today?

Colour in how high vibe you are feeling today

LOW VIBE ⟨⎯⎯⎯⎯⎯⎯⎯⎯⎯⎯⎯⎯⎯⎯⎯⎯⟩ **HIGH VIBE**

No matter how big or small . . .

What is a blessing in disguise I am grateful for?

_____

_____

_____

MY MANIFESTO

_____

_____

_____

_____

Today I have done the below to support my journey . . .

VISUALIZE ●   SELF-CARE ●   POSITIVE TALK ●

Today I need to let go of . . .

_____

_____

. . . to help me manifest.

I AM KIND

What is my vibe like today?

Colour in how high vibe you are feeling today

LOW VIBE ⟨⎯⎯⎯⎯⎯⎯⎯⎯⎯⎯⎯⎯⎯⎯⎯⎯⎯⎯⟩ **HIGH VIBE**

No matter how big or small . . .

Something I really love watching is . . .

_____

_____

_____

MY MANIFESTO

_____

_____

_____

_____

Today I have done the below to support my journey . . .

VISUALIZE ●   SELF-CARE ●   POSITIVE TALK ●

Today I need to let go of . . .

_____

_____

. . . to help me manifest.

I AM MASTERFUL

What is my vibe like today?

Colour in how high vibe you are feeling today

LOW VIBE ⟨──────────────────────⟩ **HIGH VIBE**

No matter how big or small . . .

A time when I felt a sense of gratitude for something I have was . . .

_____

_____

_____

MY MANIFESTO

_____

_____

_____

_____

Today I have done the below to support my journey . . .

VISUALIZE ●   SELF-CARE ●   POSITIVE TALK ●

Today I need to let go of . . .

_____

_____

. . . to help me manifest.

MY SELF-LOVE LIST

 It is important to nurture your needs, even if that means slowing down. Here is your chance to list everything you love to do to unwind and show up for yourself in the ways that make you feel loved.

- _____
- _____
- _____
- _____
- _____
- _____
- _____
- _____
- _____
- _____
- _____
- _____
- _____
- _____
- _____
- _____
- _____
- _____

MY REFLECTIONS

WHAT MANIFESTING PRACTICE HAS HELPED ME THE MOST?

DID I EXPERIENCE ANY OBSTACLES OR CHALLENGES?

I AM PROUD OF MYSELF BECAUSE . . .

HOW DID I STAY POSITIVE AND MAINTAIN A HIGH VIBE?

AN IMPORTANT DECISION I MADE WAS . . .

MY REFLECTIONS

I WISH I DID MORE OF . . .

I WISH I DID LESS OF . . .

WERE THERE ANY LIFE-CHANGING MOMENTS FOR ME?

NOW THE BIG QUESTION . . . WHAT'S NEXT?

NOTES

NOTES

THE UNIVERSE HAS MY BACK